DELIVERANCE PROTOCOLS & ETHICS

A Handbook for Accurate Deliverance Operations

Jennifer LeClaire

Best-Selling Author of Prophetic Protocols & Ethics

DELIVERANCE PROTOCOLS & ETHICS
A HANDBOOK FOR ACCURATE DELIVERANCE
OPERATIONS
Copyright © Jennifer LeClaire 2021

Unless otherwise noted, Scripture quotations are taken from the Modern English Version of the Bible.

Jennifer LeClaire's books are available at most Christian bookstores.
Published by Awakening Media
P.O. Box 30563
Fort Lauderdale, FL 33301
www.jenniferleclaire.org

TABLE OF CONTENTS

DEDICATION

This book is dedicated to the pioneers of deliverance, including Derek Prince, Lester Sumrall, and Frank and Ida Hammond. I am grateful for their work in bring forth present day truth for deliverance ministers and hope this book adds value to the new era of deliverance ministry.

1

A PROPHETIC WORD ABOUT DELIVERANCE MINISTERS

I've been casting out devils for decades, but when the Holy Spirit started speaking to me about a season of deliverance at my church, Awakening House of Prayer in Ft. Lauderdale, we started pressing in hard to see the captives set free.

I taught for weeks on freedom for the soul, held an inner healing intensive, a mass deliverance service, and committed to raising up deliverance ministers through the School of Deliverance at *www.schoolofthespirit.tv*.

Put another way, I started aggressively pursuing the will of God for the next stage of my ministry. During that season, I also started equipping the Body through social media. While sharing on a Facebook Live about reasons more pastors don't embrace deliverance ministry—right at the end of the broadcast—I had an unction to prophesy. I heard the Lord say:

"I am raising up even now, in your midst, a new generation and a new breed of deliverance ministers. And they will be bold like lions. They will not shrink back nor will they be intimidated by the tactics of the enemy.

"For I am putting new mantles on my deliverance ministers who are willing to take the tough cases; who are willing to go where others will not venture.

"And I am going to give them new revelations and new flows of My anointing. New rivers will flow out of them as I pour My anointing into them. And they will see even clearly inside bodies what is going on, where the stronghold is. They will see the names of the demons even written in the spirit, like the handwriting that was written on the wall in the days of Daniel.

"And they will cooperate one with another; they will become companies of deliverance ministers who will run together. They will share intelligence, and they will cooperate with one another for My glory.

"For there will not be a strong competition in the realm of deliverance as we see even now in the realm of the apostolic and in the realm of the prophetic, because these ministers have set themselves apart and they understand the need for clean hands and a pure heart.

"So, they will celebrate with one another and celebrate each other and they will relish over their victories over the kingdom of darkness together. And they will network together, not in the sense of building their own kingdom, but in order to share the stories of glory from My Spirit in the realm of deliverance.

"I am doing a new thing in deliverance ministry. Have you not yet heard about it? Well, I am announcing it to you even now in a bold way. Begin to watch and begin to pray. But also, know and recognize that many will come and try to take this new mantle—this new time and season of deliverance ministers rising up—as a fad and a trend. And they will try to hook their wagon to the greater wagon and try to use the momentum of the tide and the flow that I am bringing to the body of Christ.

"But, they will not carry the authority because their heart is compromised. They will not carry the authority that the pure ones do because they are not in it for the right reasons, and they will end up like the sons of Sceva because I don't know these ones—not the way that I need to know them—because they kept a part of their heart back from Me.

"And watch as the false deliverers arise, needing deliverance themselves. And you will see and know that I will sweep through the body of Christ and I will do a new thing in deliverance ministry in this hour."

2

WHAT ARE DELIVERANCE
PROTOCOLS & ETHICS?

You might ask, "What are deliverance protocols and ethics?" It's a good question. A protocol is a code prescribing strict adherence to correct etiquette and precedence, according to *Merriam-Webster*'s dictionary. A protocol outlines the correct way something should be done.

Yes, there is a right way to do deliverance. There are many ways. There's more than one right way, but there is a right way. Consider that precedence is part of the definition of protocols.

Precedence is how things have been done, the way things have worked in the past. When attorneys argue legal cases and when judges rule, they look to precedents to help guide them to a right decision.

Some deliverance ministers try to improve on Christ's deliverance ministry. Don't get me wrong. I understand that not everything Jesus did regarding deliverance—or any other type of miracle—is written in the pages of the Bible. I've even prophesied about new deliverance technologies. The Holy Spirit may lead you to do something you never saw demonstrated in the Bible or elsewhere. But our attitude should not be to outdo Jesus—or anybody else.

I'm not writing a rule book on protocols in the sense that I alone have all the answers on how things should be done, but it is helpful to have guidelines and standards. The Holy Spirit may lead you to break some of the protocols listed in this book for various reasons, but it would likely be rare.

Ethics are different than protocols. What are ethics? *Merriam-Webster* defines ethics as, "the discipline dealing with what is good and bad and with moral duty and obligation; a set of moral principles : a theory or system of moral values, the principles of conduct governing an individual or a group, a guiding philosophy, a consciousness of moral importance."

So protocols are the guidelines for safe, effective and lasting deliverance. Ethics are the boundaries of what is right. Just because a method of deliverance is effective doesn't make it ethical. You can get money from robbing a bank, that doesn't make it ethical. You can become a doctor by cheating on your exams, but that doesn't make it ethical. You can write a book by plagiarism, but that doesn't make it ethical.

Some of these protocols were taught to me. Others the Holy Spirit taught me directly through decades of experience in deliverance ministry. Some of these protocols are what I would call always-dos. Some of the protocols are only necessary on rare occasions but we need to cover them because when you are in the throes of deliverance, you may not otherwise know what to do.

Over the years, I've experienced some hairy, difficult deliverance sessions. It's likely as you engage in deliverance ministry at any level of frequency, the Holy Spirit will show you protocols not listed here, or ways you can adapt what I've offered for more practical use in your deliverance ministry without crossing ethical boundary lines.

That's why it's important to expose yourself to different reputable deliverance teachings. The deliverance ministry ethics I've offered in this book are absolutely non-negotiable.

3

DO WE REALLY NEED SO MANY PROTOCOLS?

From observing both legitimate and extreme deliverance ministries, and with a new generation of deliverance ministers rising up, it's clear we need deliverance ministry protocols. I am a member of the International Society of Deliverance ministers and was asked to teach on protocols at their annual conference some years ago for that reason.

Deliverance ministry protocols and ethics are vital to deliverance ministry to ensure your endeavors are safe, effective, and lasting. Deliverance ministry has seen and continues to see practices that are not safe, not effective, not lasting—and downright abusive and extreme because of a lack of training, a self-promotional mindset, greed motives and spiritual abuse.

Deliverance ministry protocols and ethics help ensure deliverance—the process of casting out demons—are safe for both the deliverance ministers and the clients. (Throughout the course of this book, we will refer to the subject of deliverance ministry as the client.) Deliverance can be dangerous for all parties if certain protocols are not followed. That danger can come in the form of physical, emotional or spiritual harm. Let's take a look at each of these aspects.

Deliverance Minister, Do No Harm
Just as God is three in one—Father, Son and Holy Spirit—man is a three-part being, spirit, soul and body. In 1 Thessalonians 5:23, Paul wrote, "Now may the God of peace Himself sanctify you completely; and may your whole spirit, soul, and body be preserved blameless at the coming of our Lord Jesus Christ."

Like physicians, we must seek to heal, not wound. There are three areas in which we can do more harm than good in deliverance ministry if we don't understand how to flow with the Holy Spirit, which means understanding the ways of God and adhering to wise protocols, especially when we don't know what to do. Those three areas of harm are physical harm, emotional harm and spiritual harm.

Physical harm occurs when a client becomes aggressive or violent, lashing out at the deliverance ministers or harming themselves either purposely or accidentally while under the influence of demons during a deliverance session. There have been unfortunate incidents of deliverance ministers restraining a client who is manifesting too forcefully, even slapping and punching a person in the name of exorcising a demon. This is unethical.

Emotional harm can occur when deliverance ministers push too far, fail to listen carefully, fail to adhere to appropriate emotional boundaries, or fail to follow through with subsequent necessary deliverance sessions. For example, there have been accounts of deliverance ministers verbally abusing clients, leaving clients hopeless in the wake of a stalled deliverance, or even developing soul ties with clients due to violating common sense ethical boundaries.

Spiritual harm can occur in a deliverance session through false deliverance ministers who impart demons to clients in an effort to make it appear they experienced a true deliverance. In this instance, the false deliverance minister is operating in divination and witchcraft and releasing a higher-ranking demon to subdue the lower ranking demon the client is struggling with. For a season, the client feels some relief but walks off worse in the long-term. Spiritual harm can also come to the deliverance minister through backlash or transference of spirits, if the minister is not aware of spiritual warfare and sanctification processes.

Establishing Effective Processes

The goal is effective deliverance ministry. When something is effective, by definition that means it is "producing a decided, decisive, or desired effect" according to *Merriam-Webster*'s.

Anything that is not effective is, by default, ineffective, which the dictionary defines as "not producing an intended effect." If we have an ineffective deliverance ministry, we can leave people hopeless, even distraught.

As deliverance ministers, we don't want to walk someone through a deliverance session without results, even though we may not see the full breakthrough in a single session. It's frustrating and disappointing for someone to come in for a deliverance session and leave without any change.

Although some deliverance sessions do not produce immediate, dramatic visible results, a client who has experienced even some noticeable measure of deliverance will not leave the same way they come in. At the least, the deliverance minister can give them hope that progress was made.

Ineffective deliverance ministry shakes people's confidence in the process and the enemy begins to convince the client they will never get free. Many people have come to me saying, "I have been here, there and everywhere and they could not cast this demon out. You are my last hope." That's a lot of pressure on the deliverance minister who gets the hard case because the last deliverance ministers were not effective.

Of course, it's not always the deliverance minister's fault. Sometimes it's the client who did not cooperate fully with the process at another ministry, or who went back into the same sin that opened the door to the demon in the first place. But an effective deliverance minister will not give up so easily because Christ-driven deliverance ministers hate to see people oppressed of the devil. Jesus went about doing good and healing all who were oppressed of the devil (see Acts 10:28). That is our aim.

Some clients have run into people who call themselves deliverance ministers but have no training. They know how to say "come out" but they don't understand their authority or operate in proper protocols and ethics and they are making messes for legitimate deliverance ministers to clean up.

Lasting Deliverance is the Aim

The goal is lasting deliverance. That means we are not just casting out demons, we are ensuring that the client is equipped to walk out the deliverance. Some deliverance ministries cast out demons and send people packing. This is not wisdom.

We know some clients will lose their deliverance because they did not follow proper after-care protocols that help slam the door on the enemy that's looking for a way back in. Post-care is critical in deliverance just as it is with surgery, or even simple piercings.

Just as it's possible for someone to get an infection in a piercing because they did not keep the area clean or to lose their healing because they did not renew their mind or reject symptoms that reappear after a healing manifests, people you deliver can end up demonized again. However, as far as it depends on the deliverance minister, we need to aim for maximum efficacy.

The client needs to understand the dynamics of deliverance and how to walk in enduring deliverance. The enemy is always looking for a way back in and if clients are not aware of this "risk of infection" they may open the door back up and be worse off than when they first came in for deliverance. Just like the late Kenneth E. Hagin taught people how to keep their healing, we need to teach people how to keep their deliverance as part of the process.

When we treat deliverance like an assembly line, we are potentially ineffective. It would be no different than a surgeon performing surgery and then sending the patient home the next day without any instructions when they are vulnerable to infection or relapse. Jesus put it this way in Matthew 12:43-45:

"When an unclean spirit goes out of a man, he goes through dry places, seeking rest, and finds none. Then he says, 'I will return to my house from which I came.' And when he comes, he finds it empty, swept, and put in order. Then he goes and takes with him seven other spirits more wicked than himself, and they enter and dwell there; and the last state of that man is worse than the first."

4

DELIVERANCE MINISTRY ETHICS, ABUSES & EXTREMES

S atan can't cast out Satan and if we hope to be effective as deliverance ministers, we need to do deliverance in the spirit of Christ; not in the spirit of greed, showmanship or any other spirit. We know deliverance ministry can be conducted by people with wrong motives or wrong relationships to Christ. Acts 19:13-16 makes this plain:

"Then some of the itinerant Jewish exorcists took it upon themselves to call the name of the

Lord Jesus over those who had evil spirits, saying, "We exorcise you by the Jesus whom Paul preaches." Also there were seven sons of Sceva, a Jewish chief priest, who did so. And the evil spirit answered and said, "Jesus I know, and Paul I know; but who are you?" Then the man in whom the evil spirit was leaped on them, overpowered them, and prevailed against them, so that they fled out of that house naked and wounded."

With this group, their motives were right but they were not equipped and probably caused more harm than good. Some deliverance ministers are sincere in their motives but they are sincerely wrong in their methods and can do damage. But there's a second group. I prophesied about a new breed of deliverance ministers in September. At the end of that prophesy, God said:

"But also, know and recognize that many will come and try to take this new mantle—this new time and season of deliverance ministers rising up—as a fad and a trend. And they will try to hook their wagon to the greater wagon and try to use the momentum of the tide and the flow that I am bringing to the body of Christ.

"But, they will not carry the authority because their heart is compromised. They will not carry the authority that the pure ones do because they are not in it for the right reasons, and they will end up like the sons of Sceva because I don't know these ones—not the way that I need to know them—because they kept a part of their heart back from Me. And watch as the false deliverers arise, needing deliverance themselves. And you will see and know that I will sweep through the body of Christ and I will do a new thing in deliverance ministry in this hour."

Remember what Jesus said in Matthew 7:21-23, "Not everyone who says to Me, 'Lord, Lord,' shall enter the kingdom of heaven, but he who does the will of My Father in heaven. Many will say to Me in that day, 'Lord, Lord, have we not prophesied in Your name, cast out demons in Your name, and done many wonders in Your name?' And then I will declare to them, 'I never knew you; depart from Me, you who practice lawlessness!'

The Message translation puts it this way "Knowing the correct password—saying 'Master, Master,' for instance—isn't going to get you anywhere with me. What is required is serious obedience—doing what my Father wills. I can see it now—at the Final Judgment thousands strutting up to me and saying, 'Master, we preached the Message, we bashed the demons, our God-sponsored projects had everyone talking.' And do you know what I am going to say? 'You missed the boat. All you did was use me to make yourselves important. You don't impress me one bit. You're out of here.'"

God forbid.

5

HOW TO USE THIS BOOK

This book is meant to offer guidelines for safe and effective deliverance ministry. It's not meant to restrain or constrain your deliverance flow or give you a rule book to criticize others in a legalistic spirit, or to lead you into the paralysis by analysis. This book aims to help you protect the integrity of your deliverance ministry by avoiding pitfalls others, even very reputable deliverance ministers, have fallen into headlong.

This book is meant to help you remember, in the heat of deliverance, some of what you already know, or teach you what to do in situations you've never seen before. I hope this book helps you come up higher in the way you walk in your deliverance anointing and gain more confidence in deliverance operations.

I would suggest reading the book through from beginning to end. Generally speaking, the protocols are outlined in a natural order of progression based on how you might encounter the client, at least in the beginning. They are all important, some are critical. This is not meant to be an exhaustive list. You may think of something practical I've left out, though it is very thorough.

You may need to read this over and over again to remember some of what you need to learn for various situations in which you find yourself. You might also find yourself referring back to it for yourself or to teach others. At the same time, depending on your level and frequency of deliverance ministry, some of these protocols may never apply to your clients.

I am not Moses. I am not laying down the deliverance law. The spirit of this book is to help you rise up and be as accurate, diplomatic and Christlike as possible. Jesus is our prototype Deliverer. We should ultimately model our deliverance ministry after His. Beyond this helpful book on protocols, I urge you to study the deliverance ministry of Christ.

PROTOCOL 1
KNOW YOUR AUTHORITY IN CHRIST

Jesus commands us to cast out devils in Matthew 10:8, "As you go, preach, saying, 'The kingdom of heaven is at hand.' Heal the sick, cleanse the lepers, raise the dead, and cast out demons. Freely you have received, freely give."

But before you engage in deliverance ministry, you need a revelation of who you are in Christ and your authority in Christ. If you don't know who you are in Christ, you are going to end up like the sons of Sceva—busted up, wounded and naked and ashamed. In case you aren't' familiar with the sons of Sceva, let me remind you of the account in Acts 19:13-16:

"Then some of the itinerant Jewish exorcists took it upon themselves to call the name of the Lord Jesus over those who had evil spirits, saying, "We exorcise you by the Jesus whom Paul preaches." Also there were seven sons of Sceva, a Jewish chief priest, who did so. And the evil spirit answered and said, 'Jesus I know, and Paul I know; but who are you?' Then the man in whom the evil spirit was leaped on them, overpowered them, and prevailed against them, so that they fled out of that house naked and wounded."

The sons of Sceva weren't in Christ and they didn't have the authority to cast out demons in His name. The Bible says, "they took it upon themselves." I don't even want to imagine that scene. I have seen demons toy with people.

I've seen demons call out people's sins, tell them their breath stinks, make fun of how they look and otherwise send them on rabbit trails with lies about what their name is. If you don't understand protocols and ethics of deliverance ministry and the devil starts taunting you and teasing you, it could shake you and you could respond wrongly.

Even if the sons of Sceva sincerely worked to obey Christ's charge to cast out devils, they didn't have the revelation of Christ, the relationship with Christ or the delegated authority from Christ to get the job done. If you want to be a safe, effective deliverance minister that drives lasting results, you need to know

Him, know who He is in you, and understand your authority in Him.

You won't have much success casting out demons if you are afraid of them or don't understand your authority. It's important to fully understand Luke 10:19, in which Jesus said, "Look, I give you authority to trample on serpents and scorpions, and over all the power of the enemy. And nothing shall by any means hurt you."

Serpents and scorpions are symbols of evil spirits and demonic powers. The word "authority" in that verse comes from the Greek word "exousia," which means "power, authority, and weight." *Merriam-Webster*'s dictionary defines "authority" as the power to give orders or make decisions: "the power or right to direct or control someone or something; the confident quality of someone who knows a lot about something or who is respected or obeyed by other people; a quality that makes something seem true or real."

Entire books have been written about the believer's authority. I recommend Kenneth E. Hagin's book titled, *The Believer's Authority*.

PROTOCOL 2
BE A STUDENT OF DELIVERANCE

The foundation of deliverance ministry is discerning the demon and casting it out. That said, deliverance ministry is accomplished in many ways. Inner healing and deliverance, for example, can go hand in hand. Every deliverance minister should understand the aspects of inner healing. Sometimes, deliverance can't occur until inner healing takes place and sometimes inner healing can't occur until deliverance takes place.

You should also be aware of how demons enter someone's mind and body, the effects of trauma as it relates to the need for deliverance and generational curses. You can enroll in the School of Deliverance or take individual deliverance classes in areas in which you are not as familiar at www.schoolofthespirit.tv.

Also, know what the Word of God says about deliverance and generational curses. Paul the apostle put it this way, "Be diligent to present yourself approved to God, a worker who does not need to be ashamed, rightly dividing the word of truth" (2 Timothy 2:15). Study Jesus as Deliverer.

Read accounts of deliverances from the late and great generals of deliverance such as Lester Sumrall, Derek Prince and Frank Hammond. Be careful about some of the newer deliverance ministries rising up, some of which are in error or overly flamboyant in making a show of deliverance.

PROTOCOL 3
DELIVERER, DELIVER THYSELF

Deliverer, deliver thyself. Before we allow people on our deliverance teams at Awakening House of Prayer, we require them to go through deliverance ministry.

Many times, nothing comes of the session because the potential deliverance minister has already dealt with the demons of their past. Other times, however, the would-be deliverance ministers have known issues or unknown common ground with the enemy that could hinder their ability to minister deliverance or even bring unnecessary warfare into their life.

There are many theories about a Christian's need for deliverance. Some believe we can never totally be delivered from demons—that we are being progressively delivered from demons until Jesus comes back. Others, however, think

Christians can be completely set free. I fall in the latter camp.

That said, if you've been through trials, hurts and wounds, traumatic events, etc. since you last got delivered, you may want to get with the Lord and ask him: "Lord, deliver me from evil, deliver me from this hurt." You don't want any common ground with the enemy. It can be difficult, for example, to cast the spirit of rejection out of someone when you are hosting a spirit of rejection. I'm not saying it can't be done, but there may be obstacles in doing so. For starters, you may not even discern the demon because of your familiarity with it.

The bottom line is this: It's more difficult to operate in the fullness of your deliverance anointing until you sever ties with the demons that bind you. Not to mention, it's not a good witness, as a deliverance minister, to walk around bound in the spirit and potentially manifesting emotional issues without even knowing it.

PROTOCOL 4
SHARPEN YOUR
SPIRITUAL WARFARE SKILLS

Take the time to become well-versed in spiritual warfare before engaging in deliverance ministry. Spiritual warfare can and often does manifest before and during deliverance sessions and there is often retaliation after the session.

Understand the weapons of your warfare, which are not carnal but mighty in God to pull down strongholds (see 2 Corinthians 10:4). Understand the concepts of binding demons, including the strongman. Jesus said, "Or how can one enter a strong man's house and plunder his goods, unless he first binds the strong man? And then he will plunder his house" (Matthew 12:19).

Understand how to loose angels to protect and war. Jesus said, "And I will give you the keys of the kingdom of heaven, and whatever you bind on earth will be bound in heaven, and whatever you loose on earth will be loosed in heaven" (Matthew 16:19).

Understand how to cast down imaginations because the enemy may attack your mind during deliverance to discourage you from continuing (see 2 Corinthians 10:5).

Understand your armor and how to wield the sword of the Spirit so you can stand against the wiles of the enemy, according to Ephesians 6:14-18:

"Stand therefore, having girded your waist with truth, having put on the breastplate of righteousness, and having shod your feet with the preparation of the gospel of peace; above all, taking the shield of faith with which you will be able to quench all the fiery darts of the wicked one. And take the helmet of salvation, and the sword of the Spirit, which is the word of God; praying always with all prayer and supplication in the Spirit, being watchful to this end with all perseverance and supplication for all the saints."

You can find the School of Spiritual Warfare at *schoolofthespirit.tv/warfareschool*.

PROTOCOL 5
CREATE A DELIVERANCE
INTAKE QUESTIONNAIRE

Most deliverance ministries choose to use some kind of deliverance intake questionnaire. You might compare it to medical history forms patients are required to fill out before they see the doctor. The physician requires this, in part, because they want to understand issues in your family line that may be causing or could cause illness.

Deliverance intake questionnaires are designed to determine the client's past and current struggles, potential generational curses and events that may have caused trauma. Our ministry uses extensive digital and written deliverance questionnaires that aim to cover anything and everything we've experienced. It's quite extensive on purpose.

Deliverance should be marked by Holy Spirit discernment but when you see someone's deliverance intake form and what they have been through, or what is in their family history, it can help you cut to the chase a lot faster, or at least give you a starting point.

Keep in mind some people are not completely honest in their intake form because of shame. Therefore, while it's a strategic tool, it's an imperfect one. We need the Holy Spirit.

Likewise, people don't always remember traumas they experienced. That's the nature of trauma. People don't always know what curses are in their family line. There are hidden curses. The bottom line is people don't always know what their issues are. So, again, the deliverance intake questionnaire is not a perfect solution but it is a strong tool.

Many times a thorough deliverance intake questionnaire itself spurs memories that are helpful to bringing the client to freedom in Christ through the leadership of the Holy Spirit. In other words, sometimes being confronted with the questions that are on the form prompts them to remember what they forgot. Some deliverance ministries do not use intake forms, but it's wisdom.

You can find a sample deliverance form in the appendix of this book.

PROTOCOL 6
RECRUITING YOUR
DELIVERANCE TEAM

If you are going to conduct deliverance ministry with any regularity, you need a deliverance team. It's important for deliverance ministers to raise up more deliverance ministers because the need for this freedom ministry is so great. That means recruiting deliverance ministry trainees.

You can start by casting vision in your local church. Who is interested in the ministry of deliverance?

Of course, just because someone is interested in joining the deliverance team doesn't mean they can automatically be onboarded. You have to get to know them. And they have to be trained. But if you don't start looking for help, you may be overwhelmed with the caseload.

Jesus recruited His deliverance ministers. He recruited the twelve and then He recruited seventy more. One example is in Mark 1:16-18, "And as He walked by the Sea of Galilee, He saw Simon and Andrew his brother casting a net into the sea; for they were fishermen. Then Jesus said to them, 'Follow Me, and I will make you become fishers of men.' They immediately left their nets and followed Him."

And, consider this, Jesus recruited you, didn't He? Here are some tips on recruiting deliverance ministers. First, cast the vision for your deliverance ministry. In your recruiting, look for people who have discernment, are grounded in the Word, and can work well on teams. Do not recruit brand new believers who have little to no experience with God or the enemy.

Once you've gathered people who are interested in learning, set forth the qualifications and expectations of joining the team, including the requirement to go through deliverance and training. Make it plain how critical deliverance ministry is, as well as both the victories and challenges of being used to set the captives free, such as backlash from the enemy. Finally, encourage them to pray about their commitment.

PROTOCOL 7
TRAIN YOUR DELIVERANCE TEAM

Beyond going through your deliverance as described in Protocol 3, you will need to equip your deliverance ministers for ministry. Your deliverance team should be competent before leading a session themselves.

In the medical world, the approach is see one, do one, teach one. But in reality surgical interns do a lot more watching before they ever hold a scalpel. Deliverance trainees should have observed several of your ministry's deliverance sessions before assisting, and worked with a team leader in dozens of sessions before leading one on their own.

Even if they have experience casting out demons it's important trainees understand your doctrine and protocols before they engage in deliverance ministry under your banner. If they have odd practices or strange ways, it will reflect poorly on your ministry.

You can do live training for each new cohort of deliverance team trainees, or do the live training once and require future deliverance team members to watch the videos. Paul told Timothy we should train people in the Word so they may be "thoroughly equipped for every good work" (2 Timothy 3:17). Equipping people for the work of deliverance ministry roots out the devil and builds up the body of Christ (see Ephesians 4:12-13).

You can also do simulations in your training, which help deliverance ministry trainees discern and learn how to handle specific situations. If you don't have training materials in house, consider investing in tools that make it easier to streamline your equipping processes.

PROTOCOL 8
DON'T TRY TO IMPROVE ON
CHRIST'S DELIVERANCE METHODS

D on't try to improve on the deliverance ministry of Christ. The Holy Spirit may lead you to do things you don't see in the Bible, as everything Jesus did is not included in the Bible. But your attitude should be to submit to the Word and the Spirit. Jesus' deliverance ministry was 100 percent successful, so don't try to improve on a perfectly perfect ministry.

Make sure you are biblical in your deliverance ministry, if not scriptural. By that I mean, your practices should line up with the spirit of the Word of God. The Spirit and the Word agree (see 1 John 5:8). If your methods violate Scripture, it will eventually discredit your ministry and probably won't be safe, effective and lasting for the client.

Again, you won't find a Scripture for everything but your deliverance techniques should be in line with the Bible. Jesus said, "Remember the word that I said to you, 'A servant is not greater than his master'" (John 15:20). Essentially, we can't do deliverance ministry better than Jesus.

Even Jesus' disciples failed to cast a spirit of epilepsy out of a boy, but Jesus never failed to make the devil flee. Not once. So we should study Christ's deliverance ministry. Yes, He had an advantage because He was sinless and full of the Holy Spirit, but He is still our model.

Debates continue over *"What did Jesus mean by greater works than these?"* It doesn't mean we are greater than Jesus. Yes, the Holy Spirit may lead you to do things that aren't in the Bible.

Jesus did a lot of miracles that were not recorded (see John 20:30). But if we want our deliverance ministry to have integrity, we need to fall in line with the ways and principles of God.

There's new language that comes with every generation in the prophetic and deliverance ministry, but they still have to be in line with the Scriptures. Christ's method of discerning the spirit and telling it to "come out" works every time.

PROTOCOL 9
QUALIFY THE CANDIDATE FOR DELIVERANCE MINISTRY

Not everyone is a qualified candidate for deliverance, though they may think they are. With regard to one-on-one scheduled deliverance sessions, be sure to qualify the candidate for deliverance before the session begins.

First and foremost, the client needs to be born again.. You can't cast out a demon from someone who is not saved. Second, they must want the deliverance. I've seen people fill out deliverance forms for family members who did not want to be free.

You can qualify a deliverance candidate by either scheduling a counseling session first or by asking the client to fill out a deliverance questionnaire. But, again, make sure the candidate actually filled out the form themselves.

Remember, although they may be experiencing demonic oppression, the reality is they may not be ready to walk through and walk out the deliverance. On the other hand, they might not need deliverance. Some people don't want to crucify their flesh and they are looking for what they think is an easy way out. Not everything is a demon.

Of course, if demons begin to manifest on the spot or if you are engaging in a mass deliverance service, this protocol goes out the window. I believe in mass deliverance services the Holy Spirit is moving on people as He wills. Sometimes when people sit under the anointing, demons will manifest and the Holy Spirit will lead me to cast them out. It's just their time. Maybe the Holy Spirit knows this is the only opportunity they will have to encounter a true deliverance ministry.

Mass deliverance and the other situations I've described are different than an extensive, intensive one-on-one deliverance session. There are still many protocols, however, that apply to mass deliverance.

PROTOCOL 10
PRAY ABOUT DELIVERANCE
ASSIGNMENTS

J ust because you have the Christ-given ability to cast out demons doesn't mean you should cast demons out of every person you run into. That's right. You don't have to and shouldn't cast out every devil out of every person you encounter, or even every person who seeks a deliverance appointment. Rather, you should pray about your deliverance ministry assignments.

Here's why: First, you need someone's permission to cast out a demon most of the time. While Paul cast the spirit of divination out of the girl of Thyatira in Acts 16, that is the exception; not the rule. I have seen people try to cast demons out of their family members who are into occult practices or other grave sin and they experience massive backlash and their "client" ended up worse than they were before.

Here's another reason: Even though the client says they want to be free, they may not be willing to do the work it takes to walk out the deliverance and maintain their freedom. For example, I've met people who want specific demons cast out but prefer to keep demons they are most familiar with.

Remember, you are not obligated to take every deliverance case that comes your way. It's okay to refuse a deliverance request if you sense you should pass. Maybe you're not ready to engage in the type or level of deliverance the client needs. Or perhaps you sense the client isn't truly able to receive from you for whatever reason, or they aren't serious about their deliverance.

Also keep in mind some clients jump from deliverance ministry to deliverance ministry seeking to test your power with no intention of repenting. These clients are not clients, they are assignments to wear you out.

Others clients jump from deliverer to deliverer because the last attempt was unsuccessful for a variety of reasons. They do what I call "the deliverance hop" just like many believers church hop. Whatever the reason, sometimes the Holy Spirit will lead you to decline a deliverance case. And that's okay.

PROTOCOL 11
MAKE SURE YOUR CLIENT

ATTENDS A LOCAL CHURCH

Before you schedule a deliverance appointment, make sure the client is plugged into a local church. Hebrews 10:24-25 tells us, "And let us consider one another in order to stir up love and good works, not forsaking the assembling of ourselves together, as is the manner of some, but exhorting one another, and so much the more as you see the Day approaching."

The idea is to ensure the person requesting deliverance has a support system in place to walk out their deliverance following the session. The person needs the prayers and support of a local church to stay free following the session.

PROTOCOL 12
OBTAINING PASTORAL PERMISSION

Whenever possible, speak to the client's pastor or get a consent letter from their church leadership before the deliverance session.

Of course, talking to or getting approval from their pastor is not always possible because, in some cases, they are too ashamed to tell their pastor what they are dealing with. We will not deny a person deliverance just because they are not comfortable enough in their local church to be honest..

In other cases, the pastor does not believe in deliverance. In still other cases, the pastors are keen on deliverance ministry but have not had the training or find that they are too close to the situation for the client to receive from them, yet unfortunately will not consent to the client obtaining deliverance from an outside ministry. Generally speaking, we encourage people to receive help in their own church. If their leadership doesn't have the capability of helping them, we encourage them to tell their pastor they are opting for help outside and get their blessing.

If the pastor won't bless the endeavor or point them to a deliverance ministry they are comfortable with, we believe the client should find another church. We will not meddle in the affairs of another pastor and his sheep by suggesting this to the client. Truth told, we don't know the whole story.

With that being said, mass deliverance services are an exception to the pastoral permission rule. We believe the Holy Spirit is moving amid mass deliverance services without anyone other than the Holy Spirit ministering to them. I often receive very specific words of knowledge at mass deliverance services that give people the faith to receive the Holy Spirit's ministry.

Mass deliverance services are typically not as in-depth as a one-on-one deliverance session. My thought is that if the Holy Spirit is the one drawing them and they are desperate for deliverance and cannot find relief in their church, the Holy Spirit will set them free from ties that bind according to His will without much direct involvement from our prayer ministers.

PROTOCOL 13
WARN THE CLIENT ABOUT
THE TEMPTATION TO FLEE

Warn the client well in advance of the deliverance session that the enemy may tempt them to run in fear, or to otherwise discourage them from coming.

One of the most common temptations is to put off the session due to busyness, even though they initially come to you in desperation seeking the deliverance ministry appointment. If you warn the client about these temptations ahead of time, they'll be prepared to resist the urge to cancel the session.

If they attempt to cancel and you discern enemy interference rather than a legitimate reason, explain to them how the devil holding them in bondage does not want them to be free because demons can't operate in the earth without bodies. Remind them of how Jesus died to set the captives free and you are honored to help them break through when they are ready.

To illustrate how this works, imagine if I told you ahead of time there are cops on a particular road. You'd likely heed the warning and not speed down that road. Likewise, when we warn people about the temptation to run away, they're less likely to fall for the temptation.

This Scripture may be helpful: "Watch and pray, lest you enter into temptation. The spirit indeed is willing, but the flesh is weak" (Matthew 26:41). You can make sure they understand their spirit is in agreement with God but their flesh is at enmity with God. Their carnal nature may agree with the demons when the pressure is on. They have to make a choice by their will to break free from oppression.

PROTOCOL 14
ASSIGN SCRIPTURE READING
BEFORE DELIVERANCE

If possible, when issues are clearly known, the client should be given Scriptures to study and prayers to pray in preparation for their ministry session. This practice helps begin the process of renewing the mind with the Word of God.

You can discern some of the client's struggles by reviewing the deliverance intake form and using your concordance to make a list of relevant Scriptures. As the client meditates on these verses, the lies holding them in bondage start getting weaker. The truth starts setting the client free before they arrive, usually making for an easier deliverance session.

For example, if the client acknowledges a struggle with rejection, prepare a sheet of Scriptures on love. In this example, you would instruct the client to meditate on God's unconditional love for them during the week before they come in.

Paul wrote, "Because the carnal mind is enmity against God; for it is not subject to the law of God, nor indeed can be" (Romans 8:7). Our minds are being renewed and where carnality remains—when the mind agrees with the flesh—it gives legal ground for the enemy to maintain its stronghold.

Again, it's God's truth that sets them free through the power of the Holy Spirit (see John 8:32). Therefore, as they begin to meditate on love (in the case of someone struggling with rejection) they're pre-conditioning their soul to receive the truth about love of God that casts out rejection. Put another way, the Word and prayer begin to loosen the grip of those demonic strongholds linked to rejection.

Biblegateway.com is a strategic tool for creating a list of scriptures—search "love" or "What does the Bible say about love?" in the app's search engine or your Internet browser. This works the same for fear, lust, pride, and other issues.

Always have the client study the Scriptures containing the truth that combats the lie. So if they are struggling with pride, for example, they would meditate on humility. If they are struggling with lust, they would meditate on holiness. Over time, you will have a collection of these Scripture and prayer sheets that you can send clients rather than having to reinvent the wheel for every client.

Whatever method you choose for Scripture and prayer preparation, do not rely on clients to do this for themselves. As deliverance ministers, we liken this process to administering a medical prescription. A pharmacy won't give you a bottle of medicine without a dosing label on it because the doctor verbally told you how many pills to take. No, the medical prescription label includes information on the dosage and instructions on how often to take the medicine.

Essentially, deliverance ministers should do everything possible to make it as easy as possible for people to get free, because the devil is going to make deliverance as laborious as he can because he wants people to stay in bondage.

PROTOCOL 15
GIVE PRIORITY TO EXTREME CASES

While, generally speaking, deliverance appointments should be on a first-come, first served basis, there are times to shake up the schedule.

If you have an active deliverance ministry, you may receive more deliverance inquiries than you can handle in any given week or month. Wisdom dictates prioritizing the most extreme cases for the sake of compassion. It's like a trauma center in a hospital. The doctors give priority to the people who are in the worst condition.

Say one client is dealing with rejection, for example, but another client is dealing with massive trauma from rape, is not sleeping at night and their marriage is struggling. Defer to the trauma case first. The person struggling with rejection is important, but the impact on their life is not as severe.

In many cases, clients have been suffering with demonic oppression for years. Waiting another week or two to deal with issues like fear or anxiety or depression will not bring them more harm. Someone tormented by traumatic memories could be tempted to harm themselves if they do not receive deliverance ministry as a priority.

PROTOCOL 16
CHOOSE THREE MINISTERS
PER SESSION

Ideally, you will have three deliverance ministers in each session: one leader, one assistant and one who is observing for training. Remember, Solomon's words in Ecclesiastes 4:12, "Though one may be overpowered by another, two can withstand him. And a threefold cord is not quickly broken."

The observer will write down what they discern and show it to the leader post-session to see if they were accurate. This model helps you to know if the trainee is ready to be an assistant. It also helps gives the trainee confidence that they are discerning accurately, as well as some level of experience in understanding what to expect.

What's more, scheduling three deliverance ministers for each session serves as a failsafe if one person suddenly has to cancel for any reason. It can be difficult to find a backup with little notice and we want to avoid having to reschedule with clients who may already be at their wits end.

PROTOCOL 17
ASSEMBLE THE RIGHT TEAM
FOR THE CLIENT

Once you have several teams, you will have the advantage of being able to assemble the right team for each client's specific case. Although people working in your deliverance ministry should adhere to your protocols, we do have to make room for style, experience and giftings.

For example, we often bring one of our pastors in for cases that appear to require some measure of inner healing. That's because pastors can be gentler and carry deep compassion that is especially helpful for people with deep hurts and wounds.

Other people may have history dealing effectively with the occult, infirmities or some other class of demons. Although any of us can cast out anything at any time in the name of Jesus under the leadership of the Holy Spirit with the client's permission, there are deliverance specialists.

Think of the medical field. There are doctors and surgeons who specialize in various practices. Some are in orthopedics. Some are in cardiology. Some are specialists in neurology. Assembling the right team for each client can maximize the results.

PROTOCOL 18
DECIDE ON SESSION LENGTHS

It's wisdom to have some protocol around the length of time you want to spend with each client. You can have a blanket protocol, such as one or two hours. Or you can determine through prayer and reading the intake form how much time is reasonable for the session.

With some time constraints, you may be better able to direct the session. For example, some people will try to take over through talking incessantly. This can be a stall tactic of the enemy or because they are nervous. If you set the session length expectation at the beginning with the team and with the client, you will not waste time that could be spent working with the next client in the waiting room.

Of course, we never want to quench the Spirit. We never want to cut off a deliverance mid-stream because the designated time is up. We always yield to what the Holy Spirit is doing. The reality is, someone can only take so much deliverance at once. Often, deliverance is like peeling an onion, so we want to make sure to follow the leadership of the Holy Spirit. He knows how much a person can take. We may conclude the session knowing there's more to deal with but you can discern when the Holy Spirit is done.

PROTOCOL 19
ESTABLISH A PROPER DRESS CODE

The deliverance team leader should set a dress code for deliverance ministers and clients. Deliverance ministers should dress modestly and comfortably, for example, because the session may be long and intense. Female deliverance ministers working with males to deliver a male client should be careful not to wear anything over which the males can stumble, such as low-cut blouses or skin tight jeans.

Women should not wear short dresses during deliverance because if the demon manifests, parts of their body may be exposed that would embarrass them later. This is not an invitation for legalism, but a practical suggestion to be comfortable and modest.

PROTOCOL 20
DEVELOP GOOD LISTENING SKILLS

You should listen carefully to the client and assure them you understand what they are saying before you commence with casting out demons. If you want the client to be a willing participant, they need to trust you. If you aren't willing to listen to their concerns and troubles, you are not demonstrating ethical deliverance.

Develop good listening skills. When you practice active listening— expressing verbal and non-verbal cues—you give clients assurance that you understand what they are saying.

A few verbal affirmations, like "uh-huh" and "I see," go a long way in establishing trust in communication. Nodding the head in agreement is another verbal cue that instills this trust. By the same token, active feedback alerts clients when you don't quite grasp what's being said. Furrowing your brow, tilting your head slightly or interjecting with a request for more details are a good means to eliminate confusion.

Since the client is clearly suffering, you want to listen with empathy. Empathetic listening will help them bring their guard down and talk freely, so you can hear what's in their heart. Jesus said, "Out of the abundance of the heart his mouth speaks" (Luke 6:45).

PROTOCOL 21
MAKE CONFIDENTIALITY CRITICAL

Confidentiality is not only key to a successful deliverance ministry—it's critical. Confidentiality means keeping a deliverance candidate's personal issues and outcomes private because the disclosure could embarrass them or bring them emotional harm.

Never share publicly what happens in a deliverance session by mentioning names or releasing videos without the person's consent. While it's helpful to use examples in teaching and training on deliverance, never share the name of the person or otherwise share information that would even accidentally reveal their identity.

Likewise, never leave deliverance forms within public reach. Keep deliverance forms in a secure locked cabinet away from prying eyes. Proverbs 12:23 assures us, "A prudent man conceals knowledge..." If your deliverance ministry has a reputation for disclosing the secrets of someone's past or the details of their oppression, you will lose credibility with God and man.

When we conduct deliverance ministry appointments, no one knows the particulars or reads forms except the deliverance ministers working on or consulting on the case. Only those who keep private information in confidence and do not gossip are allowed on our deliverance teams.

PROTOCOL 22

FASTING PRIOR TO DELIVERANCE

If possible, the deliverance team and the client should fast before the session. We know a water fast is not always feasible due to medical conditions but everyone can still do some sort of partial fast, even if it's a media fast.

When the deliverance ministers fast before seeing a client, it makes them more sensitive to the Holy Spirit. Galatians 5:16 says, "I say then: Walk in the Spirit, and you shall not fulfill the lust of the flesh." It's also true that when you crucify the flesh, you are more sensitive to the promptings of the Holy Spirit, which are vital to accomplishing a successful deliverance session. Remember this account of the disciples failing to cast out a demon of epilepsy from Matthew 17:14-21:

"And when they had come to the multitude, a man came to Him, kneeling down to Him and saying, 'Lord, have mercy on my son, for he is an epileptic and suffers severely; for he often falls into the fire and often into the water. So I brought him to Your disciples, but they could not cure him.

"Then Jesus answered and said, 'O faithless and perverse generation, how long shall I be with you? How long shall I bear with you? Bring him here to Me.' And Jesus rebuked the demon, and it came out of him; and the child was cured from that very hour.

Then the disciples came to Jesus privately and said, 'Why could we not cast it out?'

"So Jesus said to them, 'Because of your unbelief; for assuredly, I say to you, if you have faith as a mustard seed, you will say to this mountain, 'Move from here to there,' and it will move; and nothing will be impossible for you. However, this kind does not go out except by prayer and fasting."

While it's not a rule of law for deliverance ministers to fast before a session, some demons are more stubborn than others and fasting is necessary, along with much prayer in order to deal with the mechanics of the evil forces occupying a client's soul or body.

With regard to the client, fasting before deliverance prepares them for the experience. The flesh is more likely to agree with a demon force than the Holy Spirit. Remember Paul's words in Galatians 5:17:

"The sinful nature wants to do evil, which is just the opposite of what the Spirit wants. And the Spirit gives us desires that are the opposite of what the sinful nature desires. These two forces are constantly fighting each other, so you are not free to carry out your good intentions."

Fasting is demonstrating faith in God to deliver. By making our body weak, He can show Himself strong. I often say it this way, "Fasting loosens up the demons." It's sort of a spiritual lubrication. Often when people fast, the demons come out much more easily.

PROTOCOL 23
PRAY TOGETHER BEFORE
CONDUCTING DELIVERANCE

The deliverance team should come together and pray before every deliverance session. Ask the Lord to reveal demonic strongholds in the client's life. Share your insights with each other so you can be on the same page. Bind enemy interference and retaliation.

Praying together before a deliverance service is not optional. Although you typically do not have all the answers going into the deliverance session—Holy Spirit is likely to reveal other matters along the way—you want to go in with as much foreknowledge as possible. You want to have a Spirit-inspired deliverance plan to launch into deliverance ministry.

Ask the deliverance team to show up at least 30 minutes, preferably an hour, before the client to pray, worship, and go over things as a team.

PROTOCOL 24
DEALING WITH TARDY
DELIVERANCE MINISTERS

D on't allow deliverance ministers to join you mid-session unless for some reason you need backup. If the deliverance minister walks in late, they may distract the client or otherwise interrupt the session, or even quench the Spirit. Many people are already nervous coming into a deliverance session without having someone new walk in during ministry time.

Let your team know about this protocol up front. Demonstrate grace, acknowledging traffic can be heavy and other issues can arise that could cause them to legitimately be late. But train them to let you know if they are not going to make it on time so you can find a replacement minister if necessary. You want to avoid having to reschedule the appointment with a desperate person.

If someone consistently can't make it on time to the deliverance session, it's a sign that they aren't taking the responsibility seriously and should sit out until they can get control of their schedule. It may even be a character issue that could hinder the deliverance session.

Our deliverance ministry is done unto the Lord, and is an honor. Love is not rude (1 Corinthians 13:5). Consistent lateness and no shows are beyond rude, especially given the nature of the meeting.

PROTOCOL 25
DEPLOY INTERCESSORY
PRAYER BACKUP

If possible, have a team of intercessors praying in another room during the deliverance session. If that's not possible, see if you can get two or three to touch and agree on the phone from their homes.

During the deliverance session, the intercessors should cover the deliverance team and the client in prayer, pushing back darkness, binding devils, praying in the Spirit, pleading the blood of Jesus, binding retaliation, and praying as led.

When you're going into battle for someone's freedom, you need the protection over you and somebody covering you while you are doing the deliverance ministry. You are on the front lines. Ideally, you will have a few intercessors who can serve as your rear guard.

If you absolutely can't find intercessors to back you up, know that the Lord Himself can serve as your rear guard (see Isaiah 52:12) and He can also send angels to assist.

PROTOCOL 26
HAVE A WAITING ROOM

At times, you may need to ask the client to bring a friend with them especially if the person is elderly or in deep bondage. Or they may bring someone with them who wants to participate in the deliverance session.

While it can be beneficial for the client to have someone waiting for them during their session to support them afterwards, it's not suggested to let their friend or family member sit in the session for the sake of honest and private communications.

Have a waiting room or suggest a nearby restaurant or coffee shop where the friend, family member or spouse can go. You can offer to text them when the session is over. With seniors or with someone in deep bondage who is disoriented after deliverance, occasionally, it is necessary for a client to have someone waiting.

PROTOCOL 27
ASK THE CLIENT TO SIGN
A LIABILITY WAIVER

Ask the client to sign a liability form that exonerates you from any liability or injury that may occur during the deliverance session. This is a litigious society, but they can't get away with suing you for a personal injury if you have a liability form. If they will not sign a waiver of liability, it is not recommended that you proceed with the deliverance. Most likely, nothing will go wrong but it could.

PROTOCOL 28
AVOID CONFLICTS OF INTEREST

Avoid conflicts of interest at all costs. A conflict of interest is a situation in which the concerns or aims of two different parties are incompatible or a situation in which a person is in a position to derive personal benefit from actions or decisions in their official capacity, according to *Oxford Languages*.

One example of a conflict of interest could be doing one-on-one deliverance with another local pastor's sheep without their knowledge where there is a relationship present.

If you have a relationship with a local pastor and one of his members comes to you for deliverance, it would be unethical for you to keep that from the pastor. If you don't know the pastor, it is not an ethical issue to move forward but you should do so with caution and an understanding of why they can't go to their own church for deliverance.

Another example is ministering deliverance to someone with whom you have a close relationship. Hospitals do not let surgeons operate on family members for a reason. You are too close to the situation, which may make you ineffective in discerning or confronting issues that need to be addressed. The client may also not be transparent with a friend or family member in the room.

A third example is taking personal gifts or money in exchange for deliverance. While some deliverance ministries charge an administration fee that covers the cost of the employee who has to handle tasks such as paperwork and scheduling, charging for deliverance ministry or receiving gifts is not appropriate.

Remember when Elisha gave Naaman the strategy to cleanse his leprosy? The prophet would not take a personal gift. If the client chooses to make a donation to the ministry, that is acceptable but one must not take personal gifts.

Finally, anything that has the appearance of a conflict of interest must be avoided for the sake of the integrity of your deliverance ministry. Paul warned Timothy to avoid even the appearance of evil (see 1 Thessalonians 5:22).

PROTOCOL 29
KNOW YOUR BIASES

Don't minister to someone if you have a known bias or prejudice against them personally or against their race or culture. A bias is "a particular tendency, trend, inclination, feeling, or opinion, especially one that is preconceived or unreasoned; unreasonably hostile feelings or opinions about a social group; prejudice," according to *Dictionary.com*.

Studies show most biases are absolutely unconscious. Our brains are wired to find and respond to recognizable patterns, which turn into stereotypes. Catch that. Your bias is unconscious. You don't know about it or you would reject it. It's like that piece of food on your teeth that you can't see but everyone else can.

Romans 12:11 (ESV) tells us plainly, "God shows no partiality." If you are biased against a people group or you have prejudices, you need to get healed or delivered before you bring harm to a client.

PROTOCOL 30
TAKE A BREAK IF YOU ARE GOING THROUGH YOUR OWN DELIVERANCE

Don't conduct deliverance on people when you are going through deliverance yourself. In other words, if you have discovered areas in your life where you need deeper emotional healing or deliverance, you will serve your clients best by taking a break from deliverance ministry while you address those issues. There's no shame in taking a break to find your own healing or deliverance rather than ministering from a compromised position.

PROTOCOL 31
COMMIT TO THE ENTIRE PROCESS

Don't minister to someone if you cannot commit to the entire process. Don't adopt an assembly line mindset about deliverance. Deliverance is a commitment. You should prepare the client for the deliverance session as described in earlier protocols, take the time to answer questions, be ready to refer them out for counseling if you can't provide that, and offer materials that will help them walk out their deliverance.

PROTOCOL 32
AVOID GETTING TOO PERSONAL

This should go without saying, but unfortunately it has to be said. Avoid sexual relationships with people who are working through deliverance. There have been horror stories along these lines.

Likewise, do not share personal, intimate information with someone during deliverance, which could create a soul tie. Point them to Jesus. While it's okay to share how you broke through in some areas of deliverance to make them comfortable or open and give them confidence in their own victory, it's not okay to get too familiar with the client. Again, point them to Jesus. To do otherwise is unethical.

PROTOCOL 33
UNDERSTAND CULTURAL DIFFERENCES

Ethical deliverance considers the culture of the client. Beyond language, Asians, Latins and others have different cultural views and behaviors, and may respond differently in deliverance sessions. Their political opinions, values, body language, and even manifestations may be different. For example, many people in Asian nations burp when delivered.

PROTOCOL 34
DISCERN THEOLOGICAL DIFFERENCES

Denominationalism is real in the Body of Christ. Different denominations have different theologies, such as "woman can't speak in church" and cessationism—which means the gifts of the Spirit are not for today. Some denominations don't believe you can pray in tongues, or even believe praying in tongues is demonic.

If you are ministering to someone with different theological beliefs, try to respect those beliefs to the degree that you can without compromising the deliverance session or grieving the Spirit. For example, if you know a person doesn't believe in women preachers, try not to include women on the team rather than letting it offend you or offend their theology. Freedom is the goal. Paul put it this way in 1 Corinthians 9:19-22:

"For though I am free from all men, I have made myself a servant to all, that I might win the more; and to the Jews I became as a Jew, that I might win Jews; to those who are under the law, as under the law, that I might win those who are under the law; to those who are without law, as without law (not being without law toward God, but under law toward Christ), that I might win those who are without law; to the weak I became as weak, that I might win the weak. I have become all things to all men, that I might by all means save some."

That said, there may be some instances where the client's theology makes it impossible to successfully minister to them. In that case, it's better to decline the opportunity so you don't frustrate the client. You can make known your theology and see if they will still consent, or refer them elsewhere if you know your theology is a stumbling block to them.

PROTOCOL 35
REPENT BEFORE CASTING
OUT DEMONS

Make sure your own heart is clean before you go into a deliverance session. Sometimes demons will call out unrepentant sins, so repent to circumvent this encounter before you suffer unnecessary embarrassment.

Keep in mind watcher demons can spy on us, and love to catch deliverance ministers in sin. While devils aren't omnipresent or omniscient, watcher demons, also called monitoring spirits, are assigned to believers in the same way angels are assigned to believers. Repenting before deliverance cleanses you from sin that can cause demons a legal right to mock you.

That said, demons are liars and sometimes they do, at times, accuse us of sins we have not committed. This demonic agenda aims to throw us off track or to try to discredit us in front of the client or our peers. It won't rattle you if it's not true. But if it is true, it can derail the deliverance session. Therefore, repenting before engaging with demons in deliverance is wisdom.

Remember what John the apostle said in 1 John 1:9, "If we confess our sins, He is faithful and just to forgive us our sins and to cleanse us from all unrighteousness." We all sin and fall short of the glory of God, even if we don't know it. We can sin in thought, word or deed. There are sins of omission and sins of commission. Repentance is a gift.

PROTOCOL 36

RELEASE ANGELS OF DELIVERANCE

Angels are ministering spirits, sent to minister to the heirs of salvation (Hebrews 1:14). Hebrews 1:7, "And of the angels He says: 'Who makes His angels spirits And His ministers a flame of fire.'"

Angels can be helpful in deliverance, not as deliverers. Jesus is the deliverer. However, angels can help combat demon powers that are hindering the deliverance session. You can also ask angels to minister to people, like they ministered to Jesus (see Matthew 4:11). Only ask for angels to minister to people if you are led by the Holy Spirit as they obey the word of God, not our word..

I can't stress enough that angels are not deliverers. Jesus is the deliverer. We minister deliverance in His name by the power of the Holy Spirit. But we would be remiss not to, at times, call on angelic assistance in our deliverance ministry.

PROTOCOL 37
ALWAYS PRESERVE THE
CLIENT'S DIGNITY

Deliverance is serious business. People are trusting you with their past, their soul, and their dignity.

Beyond confidentiality, always preserve the client's dignity during deliverance. Dignity is showing honor and respect. The devil has already disrespected people enough. Are we going to let the devil do that on our watch?

Never do anything that would in any way compromise a client's dignity, release shame or embarrassment. Remember, do no harm.

Treat them with respect, even if they are being disrespectful. Walk in love with the person while casting out the demon. Be patient and honorable. Deliverance is not a show. Don't film them.

PROTOCOL 38
DISCERN WHEN THE CLIENT NEEDS COACHING

Sometimes, the client needs some coaching or encouragement to continue, almost like a woman giving birth to a baby. The enemy may be trying to discourage the client or they may be getting tired right on the edge of a major breakthrough.

Guide the client if you get to a blockage. Don't let them get discouraged. Coach the clients through the barrier by asking questions. Ask them what they're hearing or thinking.

Sometimes they may be too embarrassed to admit what they're hearing when shame is involved in the bondage. However, in some cases, the Holy Spirit will let you hear what they are hearing. And you can tell.

PROTOCOL 39
ELIMINATE DISTRACTIONS

Eliminate all possible natural distractions. Make sure, for example, that your private sessions are in a place without foot traffic. Make it known to anyone else in the building that you are conducting deliverance and you need privacy.

Ask the client to use the restroom before the deliverance session and avoid allowing them to bring beverages in or drink water as it could interrupt the session. Ask them to put their cell phone away and turn it on mute. That goes for the team as well. Ask them to spit out gum to avoid possible choking.

Just on the brink of freedom, we don't want the devil to talk them out of it when they are in the bathroom or because they hear the ringtone from a friend.

PROTOCOL 40
DON'T LET TOO MANY PEOPLE IN ON A DELIVERANCE SESSION

You've surely heard the saying, "Too many cooks spoil the soup." It's often the same way in deliverance ministry.

With private deliverance sessions, don't include too many people on your deliverance team for one client because it can be intimidating. Think about how you would feel if five people were there to deliver you. Three people are ideal, but you need at least two people for deliverance ministry.

In spontaneous deliverance in a public setting, such as at a mass deliverance service or at the altar, many people may rush forth to try to help. They want to be part of the process or may feel they have a word of knowledge. This is not ideal because it can overwhelm the one being delivered. Three people is plenty, as well as people to hold the drapes around them to preserve their privacy and dignity.

You'll need to assign someone to ask people to go back to their seats and pray. If a member of your deliverance team from the congregation has a word of knowledge, let them write it down and hand it to someone who is on the spontaneous deliverance ministry team for their consideration.

PROTOCOL 41
THERE IS NO FORMULA
FOR DELIVERANCE

Understand that no two deliverances will be exactly alike. Many deliverances may be fairly similar and you can learn some patterns of how demons move and how the Holy Spirit moves through experience. But you can't rely on every deliverance from fear—or any other spirit—to play out like the last one. Everyone is different.

Some deliverances are easy and some are difficult. Again, you can gain experience through deliverance ministry but don't take a cookie-cutter approach or expect the same demon to manifest exactly the same way in every person. For example, some people never have a single manifestation. Some manifest violently. Some cry the whole time. Some manifest with mocking spirits. Some are overtaken by a slumbering spirit. Some argue.

I can't stress this enough. You do gain experience in deliverance sessions but you have to be careful not to treat every client's case the same. There are nuances and the order in which you deal with strongholds may change. Fear, or any spirit, can manifest in many different ways—some of which you may have never seen. There's always more to learn. This is, again, why we rely on the leadership of the Holy Spirit.

PROTOCOL 42
MAKE SAFETY YOUR PRIORITY

The possibility for injury is real in deliverance ministry. If people begin manifesting and for some reason you are unsuccessful in binding the manifestations, safety is the immediate priority. Protect the person by keeping the environment safe, and avoid physical danger to the person and yourself.

Jesus questioned the father of a boy with a spirit of epilepsy that experienced strong manifestations: "'So He asked his father, "How long has this been happening to him?' And he said, 'From childhood. And often he has thrown him both into the fire and into the water to destroy him'" (Mark 9:21-22).

I have seen people scratch their face or bang their head on the ground, among other harmful manifestations. Unfortunately, I have also seen deliverance ministers walk away with scratches trying to keep demons from harming the client. Sometimes you may have to restrain a client who is harming themselves. Be careful not to use excess force.

PROTOCOL 43
KEEP A BIBLE ON HAND

Always have your Bible—which is your Sword—with you during a deliverance session in case you need to reference it. Sometimes, the Holy Spirit will give you a Scripture to read, so have your Bible handy. Yes, there is value and convenience with Bible apps but we don't want to pull our phones out during deliverance. That's because it could be a distraction for you if you happen to see a message pop up and it may cause the client to think you are prioritizing your personal affairs above their deliverance.

PROTOCOL 44
DEVELOP HAND SIGNALS

Consider developing some hand signals so that the demon (and the client) can't hear you communicating in the heat of the deliverance. These can be simple hand signals indicating stop, start, no, yes, do it again, hit that harder, etc. You only need a few simple hand signals that are self-explanatory.

PROTOCOL 45
USE TRANSLATORS WHEN NECESSARY

If the client speaks a different language than you, try to have a translator who is also skilled in deliverance ministry. The demons understand any language but it's important for the person to understand what is going on so they are not afraid.

In South Florida, we have a lot of Spanish speakers and people who only speak Spanish. I've cast devils out of Spanish-only speakers in mass deliverance services, but in private sessions you need a translator so the client understands what is going on and, if necessary, follow your prompts to repent or share the answers to questions you may have.

PROTOCOL 46
DON'T MINISTER BEYOND
YOUR AUTHORITY

Don't minister beyond your authority. If you don't have experience in a certain area and you don't have a backup, do not proceed without the leadership of the Holy Spirit. As deliverance ministers, we strive to help our clients but it's just as important to do them no harm. You can also do yourself harm. Remember the sons of Sceva from Acts 19:13-16, (Message):

"Some itinerant Jewish exorcists who happened to be in town at the time tried their hand at what they assumed to be Paul's 'game.' They pronounced the name of the Master Jesus over victims of evil spirits, saying, 'I command you by the Jesus preached by Paul!'

"The seven sons of a certain Sceva, a Jewish high priest, were trying to do this on a man when the evil spirit talked back: 'I know Jesus and I've heard of Paul, but who are you?' Then the possessed man went berserk—jumped the exorcists, beat them up, and tore off their clothes. Naked and bloody, they got away as best they could."

PROTOCOL 47
DON'T CAST OUT DEMONS ALONE

D on't cast out devils alone. This is not a one-person job. Jesus sent the disciples out two by two. Mark 6:7 illustrates this, "And He called the twelve to Himself, and began to send them out two by two, and gave them power over unclean spirits."

This was not a fluke. We see this same strategy again in Luke 10:1, "After these things the Lord appointed seventy others also, and sent them two by two before His face into every city and place where He Himself was about to go."

Beyond the Scriptural references to how Christ deployed deliverance ministers, there is another issue at hand. You should minister in pairs so that there is a credible witness against attempts to falsely accuse you. A false accusation, even though false, can derail your deliverance ministry. It's your word against a demonized person, but many people are so opposed to deliverance ministry that they are looking for a reason to discredit you. Don't give them one.

There are, of course, exceptions to this rule. Obviously, if someone is manifesting demons and bringing harm to themselves or others, you are a candidate for the Holy Spirit to use to diffuse the situation. He may lead you to do something about it. But that is the exception, not the rule. Never schedule a deliverance appointment alone. Use wisdom in these cases to avoid any issues. Know when to make referrals.

PROTOCOL 48
DELIVERING THE OPPOSITE SEX

You don't need all women on a team to deliver a female client. Nor do you need all men on a team to deliver a man. However, if you are ministering to a male client, a male minister needs to be on the deliverance team. Likewise, if you are ministering to a female client, a woman minister needs to be on the deliverance team.

Put another way, when ministering to someone of the opposite gender, the same gender needs to be in the mix. This is wisdom because men and women who are not related should not, typically, be behind closed doors together. The great evangelist Billy Graham lived by a gender rule: he never be alone with a woman who wasn't his wife. It is now widely known as The Billy Graham Rule.

You don't need to set yourself up for false accusations of a sexual misconduct nature. You don't need temptations. And you do need to consider safety. Demons are powerful and can bring bodily harm to someone if they catch you off guard.

PROTOCOL 49
DON'T MINISTER TO HUSBAND
AND WIFE TOGETHER

It's generally not wise to minister to a husband and wife—or two people—together. They may not be completely transparent. In regards to spouses or two people, it's good practice to schedule separate appointments.

The deliverance ministry process typically comprises sensitive issues that some may find uncomfortable to address in front of their spouse. Perhaps the wife never told the husband she was sexually assaulted because she is ashamed or afraid he will not see her the same. Perhaps the husband doesn't want confess his pornography addiction with his wife present, even if she already knows.

It is not our place to judge how transparent married couples should be with one another. It is our job to provide a safe environment, where the client can share confidential information without fear of disclosure or relational repercussions.

If the client is concealing information out of fear, it can hinder the deliverance. If someone is not being honest with you, they can't get free. The same is true for conducting deliverance on any two people together, even if they are good friends and agree or want to do it this way.

PROTOCOL 50
PRACTICAL CONSIDERATIONS

Deliverance can get messy. Many people cry and will need tissues. Some will vomit, so you need a trash can ready. Have Kleenex, paper towels and lined trash cans on hand in case they are needed. You'll be glad you did.

PROTOCOL 51
KEEP A NOTEPAD AND PEN HANDY

Have paper and pen handy in case you want to write something down or discretely pass a note to someone on the deliverance with an insight about the session, such as what demon you are discerning.

Of course, you can whisper in another deliverance team member's ear and sometimes this is the best avenue for dialogue. We've used both methods—whispering and passing notes. But there are times you don't want to announce your revelation or your doubt aloud because the enemy or the client may hear you.

It may be best to pass a note depending on the circumstance. Use your judgment but be discreet enough that the client doesn't discern you are stumped or that you team is not in agreement about where to go next.

PROTOCOL 52
HAVE SOMEONE TAKE NOTES

The trainee or observer in the deliverance ministry session should take notes, like a nurse would take notes for a doctor. The notetaker may chronicle what was cast out in case you need to keep record for future deliverances, or to share it with the client.

The trainee may also chronicle areas of resistance or other insights to share during debriefing. The trainee should always write down what they are discerning so the team leader can judge it and determine their accuracy and readiness to join as an assistant or launch their own team within your ministry.

PROTOCOL 53
MAKE THE CLIENT FEEL COMFORTABLE

Many people who come in for deliverance are anxious, nervous and afraid. It's the deliverance ministry team leader's job to make the client feel comfortable before you start the opening prayer. Greet them warmly. Assure them that you and the team are prepared and eager to help them, and that God is able to deliver them.

Explain the process and ask them if they have any questions before you begin. Sometimes if they seem especially anxious, I tell them a story about my own deliverance to put them at ease.

PROTOCOL 54
PRAY IN FRONT OF THE CLIENT

Even though you have already prayed privately, pray also in front of the client. This is sort of akin to a doctor washing his hands in front of the patient even if his hands are already clean. Pray for the gifts of the Spirit to be in operation. Invite the presence of the Lord and bind up retaliation. This builds faith in the client's heart.

PROTOCOL 55
EXPLAIN POTENTIAL MANIFESTATIONS

Explain to the client what may happen with regard to demonic manifestations so they won't be afraid if they begin to manifest. You may want to share information about manifestations that could emerge during a deliverance session, such as yawning, crying, vomiting, shaking and the like. Also explain that manifestations are not necessary to deliverance. Some people get free without a single manifestation.

The client may have heard horror stories about manifestations. I usually tell them not to be concerned with what might happen because I've seen it all. The idea is to prevent them from feeling embarrassed or ashamed over something they may not be able to control.

Instruct them ahead of time to resist the manifestations by force of their will. If they are especially demonized, however, they may black out and not know what they are doing. Explain to the deliverance client that as they resist the manifestations, you will bind them.

I teach extensively on manifestations and how to deal with them in the School of Deliverance at *www.schoolofthespirit.tv*.

PROTOCOL 56
DON'T TOUCH THE CLIENT
WITHOUT PERMISSION

Ask the client before the session starts if it's OK to touch them. You should ideally only touch them on their head, shoulders, or back, but you may at times be led to put your hand on their feet, or even stomach.

Women should not put their hands on a man's stomach and vice versa.

By requesting this permission, you are being sensitive to unhealed trauma affects like physical assault or sexual abuse. Beyond that, some people just do not like to be touched for unknown reasons. Remember, you don't have to lay hands on someone to cast a demon out.

Consider Matthew 8:16, "When evening had come, they brought to Him many who were demon-possessed. And He cast out the spirits with a word, and healed all who were sick..." The New Living Translation puts it this way: "He cast out the evil spirits with a simple command, and he healed all the sick."

PROTOCOL 57
CONFIRM THE CLIENT HAS FORGIVEN

Unforgiveness is the most strategic legal right the enemy has in a believer's life. Jesus said, Matthew 6:14: "For if you forgive men for their sins, your heavenly Father will also forgive you. But if you do not forgive men for their sins, neither will your Father forgive your sins."

Ask the Holy Spirit to show the person seeking deliverance if they need to forgive anyone. Sometimes you see evidence of unforgiveness on the deliverance intake form. But also make sure you directly ask the client before you try to start casting out demons.

Let me restate this more strongly: If the client is harboring unforgiveness in their heart, the enemy will not leave. He has a legal right. Unforgiveness affords an opportunity to the devil to keep the client in bondage (see Ephesians 4:26-27). Unforgiveness allows Satan to outwit us (see 2 Corinthians 2:10-11). It's worth including the Parable of the Unforgiving Servant here from Matthew 18:23-35. Reading this passage in Matthew 18 can help them understand one reason why they may be in such bondage.

"Therefore the kingdom of heaven is like a certain king who wanted to settle accounts with his servants. And when he had begun to settle accounts, one was brought to him who owed him ten thousand talents.

"But as he was not able to pay, his master commanded that he be sold, with his wife and children and all that he had, and that payment be made. The servant therefore fell down before him, saying, 'Master, have patience with me, and I will pay you all.' Then the master of that servant was moved with compassion, released him, and forgave him the debt.

"But that servant went out and found one of his fellow servants who owed him a hundred denarii; and he laid hands on him and took him by the throat, saying, 'Pay me what you owe!' So his fellow servant fell down at his feet and begged him, saying, 'Have patience with me, and I will pay you all.'

"And he would not, but went and threw him into prison till he should pay the debt. So when his fellow servants saw what had been done, they were very grieved, and came and told their master all that had been done. Then his master, after he had called him, said to him, 'You wicked servant! I forgave you all that debt because you begged me. Should you not also have had compassion on your fellow servant, just as I had pity on you?'

"And his master was angry, and delivered him to the torturers until he should pay all that was due to him. So My heavenly Father also will do to you if each of you, from his heart, does not forgive his brother his trespasses."

Some people insist they have forgiven everyone who wronged them, but you may discern otherwise. Some people may even have a spirit of unforgiveness. They may truly believe they have forgiven. This is where you need to press in more to the Holy Spirit to discern who or what they are holding a grudge against so you can share that word of knowledge and bring forth an aha moment for the client.

Noteworthy is the reality that sometimes the person has unforgiveness toward someone who has died and doesn't think they need to or even can forgive since they are dead. Lead them to forgive anyway. Teach them that forgiveness is to cleanse them and shut the enemy out. Forgiving is for the client's benefit not for the benefit of the one who wronged them. And remember, forgiveness does not always mean reconciliation.

Another reality is this: people often have unforgiveness toward themselves or even toward God. God never does anything that requires forgiveness. He is perfect in all of His ways (see Psalm 18:30). But people do get mad at God, harbor resentment toward Him or even become bitter. Lead them in a prayer of forgiveness to release those who hurt them.

A third reality is there could be there is a generational curse of unforgiveness in the family blood line. Still, forgiveness is an act of the client's will. They can choose to agree with God and forgive. Then the generational curse can be broken, the demons can be cast out, and the client does not have to live in torment anymore.

PROTOCOL 58
EXPLORING OTHER LEGAL RIGHTS

While unforgiveness is perhaps the most common legal right, there are other legal rights that must be explored when you hit a wall in deliverance. The overarching legal right is the practice of sin. Sin is a wide, open door for the enemy. And the deeper the sin, the wider the threshold.

Soul ties are legal rights. Soul ties are formed during sexual intercourse. 1 Corinthians 6:16 tells us plainly, "Or do you not know that he who is joined to a harlot is one body with her? For 'the two,' He says, 'shall become one flesh.'" You may have to instruct the client regarding soul ties, as many Christians are not aware of what a soul tie is.

Where soul ties, which can also be formed through strong emotional bonds, are present the demons harassing one person can harass the other. You need to educate the client about soul ties and instruct them how to break the soul tie in order to cast out the demon.

Inner vows are prime territory for demons. That's why Jesus said in Matthew 5:34-35. "But I say to you, do not swear at all: neither by heaven, for it is God's throne; nor by the earth, for it is His footstool; nor by Jerusalem, for it is the city of the great King. Nor shall you swear by your head, because you cannot make one hair white or black. But let your 'Yes' mean 'Yes,' and 'No' mean 'No.' For whatever is more than these comes from the evil one."

Inner vows often start with the words, "I will never..." or "I will always..." The enemy tempts us to make inner vows when we are vulnerable, angry, hurt or wounded. Remember, the power of death and life are in the tongue (see Proverbs 18:21). People often make these inner vows as children or in times of stress or trauma and don't remember doing it. The Holy Spirit can show you their inner vows through a word of knowledge or bring them to the client's remembrance.

Self-imposed curses also open the door to the enemy. Some people have uttered words such as, "I wish I was dead" which is essentially a death curse. This can attract all sorts of demons, including apathy, infirmity and death.

There may also be generational curses present or the client may be wearing cursed objects or have cursed objects on display in their homes. Check out my book *Deliver Your Home from Evil* for more on cursed objects.

PROTOCOL 59
LEAD THE CLIENT IN REPENTANCE

Renouncing is speaking to the enemy. Repentance is speaking to God. Lead the client to repent for any known sin, and to repent for allowing the enemy to get a foothold in their life. If it is a generational sin, lead them to repent on behalf of their family line.

Explain clearly that God is not mad at them, and that whatever allowed the enemy to get a stronghold may not be their fault. Still, repentance is required.

Here's why: The client may not have committed the sin. In reality, a sin may have been committed against them, such as abuse or exposure to trauma. But the reaction to the sin against them may have been sinful, such as holding grudges or entering into self-protection or shutting people out because of their pain.

Repentance is a gift. 1 John 1:9 tells us, "If we confess our sins, He is faithful and just to forgive us our sins and to cleanse us from all unrighteousness."

Repentance further strips the enemy of his legal rights in the client. Paul explains the power of repentance in 2 Corinthians 7:10-11:

"For godly sorrow produces repentance leading to salvation, not to be regretted; but the sorrow of the world produces death. For observe this very thing, that you sorrowed in a godly manner: What diligence it produced in you, what clearing of yourselves, what indignation, what fear, what vehement desire, what zeal, what vindication! In all things you proved yourselves to be clear in this matter."

PROTOCOL 60
LEAD THE CLIENT IN
RENOUNCING THE DEMONS

Once you've identified by the insight of the Holy Spirit what demon or demons Jesus wants to cast out first, lead the client to renounce the demons.

Renounce means "to give up, refuse, or resign usually by formal declaration; to refuse to follow, obey or recognize any further; to repudiate," according to *Merriam-Webster*'s dictionary.

When the client renounces a demon, he is breaking all agreement with the devil and its activities in their soul or flesh. The client must do this out loud because the enemy can't hear them if they say it in their head. In breaking agreement with the enemy, the legal right is severed and deliverance will follow.

Once the client submits themselves to God and resists the devil, he has to flee (see James 4:7). Renouncing is easy. Just lead them to say, "I renounce (and then list the demons).

PROTOCOL 61
DESIGNATE ONE
DELIVERANCE LEADER

One person should be designated as the leader of the deliverance session. One person and only one person can lead the charge. Your deliverance team can't have two heads. There's one senior surgeon at the operating table with many residents, interns and nurses assisting. There's one head coach on a basketball team with many assistant coaches and trainers. Schools have one principal with many teachers.

Having more than one leader brings confusion and can disrupt the flow of the Holy Spirit. That said, others on the team play a valuable role in discerning things you may miss, praying in the Spirit, waging warfare against resistance and the like.

Since there can only be one leader, others on the team should submit any revelation they receive through words of knowledge, discerning of spirits or other prophetic insight to the leader to judge rather than interrupting the flow and taking the session in a different direction.

Even if the revelation is accurate, it may not be the right time to go after the demon they are discerning. The leader is graced to judge. Even if the leader is wrong, there can be no sign of division or disorder on the team or the enemy will get in. Paul said, "Let all things be done decently and in order" (1 Corinthians 14:40).

Teach the team that the leader is the leader because they have more experience than you or because they are on a rotation and people will take turns leading. But the leader is the leader. God is going to honor that leadership.

That said, we typically allow the person who received the revelation of a stronghold to take point on casting out the demon they discerned at the right time in the session.

PROTOCOL 62
ASK THE CLIENT POINTED QUESTIONS

As the deliverance session begins, ask the person what they believe is the biggest issue or hindrance in their life. This can be revealing and get you started, but does not necessarily mean the Holy Spirit will lead you to address those concerns first, or even at all.

Sometimes the client has obtained deeper insight into the cause or source of their demonization since the time they filled out their deliverance intake questionnaire. They may have information that serves as the missing link to freedom.

I usually ask, "What do you think is your biggest issue? What really brought you today? I know you filled out the forms but what really brought you here today?" Many times, not always, the answer to this question is the strongman.

PROTOCOL 63

CAST THE DEMON OUT

Once you identify a stronghold and have led the person to renounce and repent, cast it out in the name of Jesus. I like to say "come out, in Jesus' name." Other people may say, "Loose them, in Jesus' name" or "let them go, in Jesus' name." The most important thing is that you use the name of Jesus. It is His authority under which you are operating.

Philippians 2:9-11 tells us, "Therefore God also has highly exalted Him and given Him the name which is above every name, that at the name of Jesus every knee should bow, of those in heaven, and of those on earth, and of those under the earth, and that every tongue should confess that Jesus Christ is Lord, to the glory of God the Father."
And again in Romans 14:11, "For it is written: 'As I live, says the Lord, Every knee shall bow to Me, And every tongue shall confess to God.'"

PROTOCOL 64
DISCERN GENERATIONAL CURSES

At times, there are generational curses present that need to be broken before the enemy will give up his legal rights.

The topic of generational curses is controversial in the Body of Christ. Many believe that generational curses, also known as family curses or bloodline curses, cannot be present in the life of a believer.

Some quote this scripture in Galatians 3:13, "Christ has redeemed us from the curse of the law, having become a curse for us (for it is written, "Cursed is everyone who hangs on a tree"), that the blessing of Abraham might come upon the Gentiles in Christ Jesus, that we might receive the promise of the Spirit through faith." But we see clear evidence of generational curses.

Proverbs 26:2 tells us, "Like a flitting sparrow, like a flying swallow, so a curse without cause shall not alight." Curses have to have a cause to land, and generational curses have a bloodline right.

The world says it like this, "Like father like son." The Word says it like this, "The iniquity of the father passes on from generation to generation."

Many times we translate the word "iniquity" as "sin." But it's not the sin that passes on from generation to generation. It's the curse, the penalty. A curse is a spirit that passes from generation to generation until someone finally figures out how to stop it in Jesus' name.

When Jesus was walking with His disciples, they asked if the man was blind for something he did or something his parents did. Jesus didn't rebuke them for asking a foolish question because being Jewish, they understood Ezekiel 18:2, "The fathers have eaten sour grapes but the children's teeth are set on edge." In other words, the fathers have done something but the children pay the price.

PROTOCOL 65
USE THE WORD AS A WEAPON

Deliverance ministers should be rooted and grounded in the Word of God. The Word contains truth to combat the demons that hold your client captive. Often, during deliverance sessions, speaking the Word of God out loud to the demons causes them to tremble, come out and flee. If you don't know the Word of God, you won't be able to readily quote it.

Paul told his spiritual son Timothy to, "Be diligent to present yourself approved to God, a worker who does not need to be ashamed, rightly dividing the word of truth" (2 Timothy 2:15). Applying truth in deliverance is key to dislodging stubborn demons.

Remember the truth in Hebrews 4:12, "For the word of God is living and powerful, and sharper than any two-edged sword, piercing even to the division of soul and spirit, and of joints and marrow, and is a discerner of the thoughts and intents of the heart."

Not only is the Word your sword, God can make your mouth like a sharp sword when you release His Word (see Isaiah 49:2). God's Word is like fire and a hammer that smashes enemy opposition to your deliverance client's freedom (see Jeremiah 23:29).

If you are not well-versed in the Word in certain areas, study out relevant Scriptures before you go into a deliverance session. Sow that time into your client's life. When you sow to the Spirit, you will strengthen your deliverance ministry and be a more effective minister.

PROTOCOL 66
A WORD ABOUT PRAYING
IN TONGUES

Supporting members on the deliverance team should pray in tongues quietly during the session. When you pray in tongues, you're praying the perfect prayer. Romans 8:26 tells us:

"Likewise the Spirit also helps in our weaknesses. For we do not know what we should pray for as we ought, but the Spirit Himself makes intercession for us with groanings which cannot be uttered."

When support members pray in the Spirit during the deliverance session, I believe it's unlocking wisdom, discernment and other prophetic insight needed to help see the captive set free. I also believe praying in tongues can push back darkness.

However, instruct the client not to pray in tongues during deliverance. You can't receive while you are pouring out. General wisdom is that the demons will not come out while the client is praying in tongues.

PROTOCOL 67
DON'T LET THE CLIENT
CONTROL THE SESSION

Sometimes, the client or a demon in the client will try to control the deliverance session. It may look like them telling you what their issue is and refusing any other form of ministry when there are clearly other demonic issues present beyond what they have described.

It could also be that they are wrong about or blind to the demonization that holds them in bondage and refuse to acknowledge what the Holy Spirit is showing you. They may refuse to renounce the demon you clearly see binding them. When people get into their head about deliverance, it can be difficult to work with them.

PROTOCOL 68
DON'T WORK WITH
UNCOOPERATIVE PEOPLE

Don't try to force anything in deliverance. Don't push the person further than they can go or are willing or able to go. If the client isn't willing to forgive or renounce or repent, counsel, coach them to see if they will submit to God.

If the client refuses to cooperate, eventually you have to end the session because you can't do anything without their cooperation. God doesn't work against someone's will and neither can you.

In that case, let them know that you are ready to help them when they are ready to cooperate and pray over them kindly. You may even give them some additional Scriptures to study so the Holy Spirit can shed light on the matter or bring conviction.

Never give a client ultimatums. You are there to serve. Always be led by the Holy Spirit. It is His power that delivers people in the name of Jesus.

PROTOCOL 69
DEALING WITH THE STRONGMAN AND HIS GUARDS

Many times, you can see the strongman at the outset of the deliverance session. The Holy Spirit may even show you the strongman before the session begins. Still, you have to deal with guarding demons first. If you set out to cast out the strongman straight away, you are usually unsuccessful.

Again, guarding demons typically must be cast out first. Guarding demons are less powerful demons that are often guarding a wound or a legal right you haven't uncovered. Guarding demons may also just be there to distract you from the strongman altogether. Or they could just be defending the strongman's position.

Remember, deliverance is like peeling an onion or untying a knot. You have to pull the right string first or you can make the knot tighter. This, again, is why you need to depend on the leadership of the Holy Spirit. He knows what to cast out first, then second, then third and so on. Ultimately, the person won't be completely free until you get to the strongman. This is a telling passage in Matthew 12:22-29 that's worth reading in its entirety:

"Then one was brought to Him who was demon-possessed, blind and mute; and He healed him, so that the blind and mute man both spoke and saw. And all the multitudes were amazed and said, 'Could this be the Son of David?'

"Now when the Pharisees heard it they said, 'This fellow does not cast out demons except by Beelzebub, the ruler of the demons.'

"But Jesus knew their thoughts, and said to them: 'Every kingdom divided against itself is brought to desolation, and every city or house divided against itself will not stand. If Satan casts out Satan, he is divided against himself. How then will his kingdom stand?

"And if I cast out demons by Beelzebub, by whom do your sons cast them out? Therefore they shall be your judges. But if I cast out demons by the Spirit of God, surely the kingdom of God has come upon you. Or how can one enter a strong man's house and plunder his goods, unless he first binds the strong man? And then he will plunder his house. He who is not with Me is against Me, and he who does not gather with Me scatters abroad."

When you get stuck in deliverance, one possibility is that you have run into a guarding demon that you haven't discerned. Pray about the guards and take them down so you can bind and cast out the strongman.

PROTOCOL 70
PLEAD THE BLOOD OF JESUS

At strategic times during the deliverance session, such as stalemates in the spirit or when the client begins to manifest aggressively (i.e. growling or flailing around or screaming) support ministers should plead the blood of Jesus. The devils hate to hear about the blood.

The blood of Jesus gives us remission from our sins: Matthew 26:28, "For this is My blood of the new covenant, which is shed for many for the remission of sins." Remission is to release from guilt or penalty. We were going to hell with Satan and his angels until we received the overcoming blood sacrifice of Jesus.

The blood of Jesus justifies us: Romans 5:9 says, "Much more then, having now been justified by His blood, we shall be saved from wrath through Him." When the Accuser of the Brethren attacks, the blood stands up for us.

The blood of Jesus is our mediator: Hebrews 12:24 says, "to Jesus the Mediator of the new covenant, and to the blood of sprinkling that speaks better things than that of Abel" (Hebrews 12:24). The covenant affords you many benefits, including protection from the enemy.

The blood of Jesus gives us peace: Colossians 1:20 reads, "and by Him to reconcile all things to Himself, by Him, whether things on earth or things in heaven, having made peace through the blood of His cross."

The blood of Jesus gives us access to the throne room: Hebrews 10:19-20 tells us, "Therefore, brethren, having boldness to enter the Holiest by the blood of Jesus, by a new and living way which He consecrated for us, through the veil, that is, His flesh…" We can go boldly to the throne of grace and obtain grace and mercy in the battle.

The blood of Jesus sanctifies us: Hebrews 13:12 reveals, "Therefore Jesus also, that He might sanctify the people with His own blood, suffered outside the gate." The blood purifies us and sets us apart as God's own.

The blood of Jesus forgives and cleanses us from our sin as Christians. 1 John 1:9 assures, "If we confess our sins, He is faithful and just to forgive us our sins and to cleanse us from all unrighteousness." The blood of Jesus paves the way for victory in warfare. Revelation 12:11, "And they overcame him by the blood of the Lamb and by the word of their testimony, and they did not love their lives to the death."

PROTOCOL 71
DON'T ENGAGE IN CONVERSATIONS WITH DEVILS

Don't engage in conversations with devils. This is not a show, and devils lie. There is only one time in Scripture when we see Jesus talking to the demons other than to say, "Come out." That was when He was dealing with the man from the Gadarenes. Mark 5:1-9 tells the account of this extreme deliverance case:

"Then they came to the other side of the sea, to the country of the Gadarenes. And when He had come out of the boat, immediately there met Him out of the tombs, a man with an unclean spirit, who had his dwelling among the tombs; and no one could bind him, not even with chains, because he had often been bound with shackles and chains. And the chains had been pulled apart by him, and the shackles broken in pieces; neither could anyone tame him. And always, night and day, he was in the mountains and in the tombs, crying out and cutting himself with stones.

"When he saw Jesus from afar, he ran and worshiped Him. And he cried out with a loud voice and said, "What have I to do with You, Jesus, Son of the Most High God? I implore You by God that You do not torment me.' For He said to him, 'Come out of the man, unclean spirit!' Then He asked him, 'What is your name?' And he answered, saying, 'My name is Legion; for we are many.'"

I have seen deliverance ministers on social media and on TV engaging in long, drawn-out conversations, even calling up to speak and then binding them. It's like a circus show. This compromises the dignity of the client and, in reality, puts the deliverance minister in danger. Deliverance is not a game.

There might be an occasion where God will lead you to ask the demon a question, but the devil is a liar; so you will never know if they are telling you the truth without a witness of the Holy Spirit. Long, drawn-out conversations with demons are not common practice of legitimate deliverance ministers. Satan is the father of lies (see John 8:44). Talking to demons defies Holy Spirit intelligence and can give the demon control in the session.

PROTOCOL 72
THERE'S NO NEED TO SCREAM AT THE DEVIL

I tend to be loud and aggressive against stubborn demons because of a righteous indignation and fervency in the spirit. However, if you are screaming and yelling, you could scare the client. The enemy is not deaf. He can hear you even in a whisper.

I've searched diligently, but I can't find any passage that shows Jesus losing His voice because He screamed and hollered at the devil too long. When Satan confronted Jesus in the wilderness with all manner of temptation, Jesus simply wielded the sword of the Spirit, which is the Word of God (see Ephesians 6:17).

The Bible indicates that "Jesus said, 'It is written ...'" (Matt. 4:4-10, emphasis added)—not that Jesus yelled, Jesus hollered, Jesus screamed or Jesus shouted in frustration. Jesus said God's Word and let the Word cut through Satan's lies.

Likewise, when Jesus cast out devils, He didn't scream at them. It was the demons, rather, who were screaming. When Jesus cast out the demons from the two men in the Gadarenes, He simply said, "Go!" (see Matthew 8:32). When Jesus cast out a demon in the synagogue, He calmly said, "Be quiet, and come out of Him!" (Luke 4:35). And when Jesus cast the demon out of the epileptic boy, He just rebuked the demon and it took off (see Matthew 17:18).

We don't need to scream at the devil—and more volume doesn't equal more power. We just need to stand in our authority in Christ.

PROTOCOL 73
MAINTAIN YOUR COMPOSURE
UNDER PRESSURE

Don't let the devil see you sweat if you are stumped or meet with a difficult confrontation. Keep it together and remain grounded in your authority even when you feel unsure of what to do next.

It's possible the demonized person will get physically aggressive or even get in your face or lunge at you. You may feel physically threatened. Remember, you have authority over all the power of the devil. If you lose your composure, the enemy knows you are not confident in your identity in Christ or in your spiritual warfare skills.

Paul the apostle said, "and not in any way terrified by your adversaries, which is to them a proof of perdition, but to you of salvation, and that from God" (Philippians 1:28). The Message translation puts it this way: "Not flinching or dodging in the slightest before the opposition. Your courage and unity will show them what they're up against."

PROTOCOL 74
DON'T LET MANIFESTATIONS DISTRACT YOU

If you engage in deliverance frequently, you'll see many strange manifestations just like doctors who work in trauma centers see strange injuries.

A demonic manifestation is best explained as evidence that a demon is present in or on a person. A demonic manifestation may be subtle and discerned through experience, but demonic manifestations are perceived with the senses, particularly sight. A demonic manifestation is essentially the enemy showing himself and revealing his presence.

Sometimes, demonic manifestations can be unsettling, violent, or even pornographic. Don't get distracted by the manifestations. Bind them and preserve the dignity of the person.

PROTOCOL 75
DON'T FORCE MANIFESTATIONS

I've seen more than one deliverance minister force manifestations. This is a mistake. Forced manifestations do not drive effective, safe and lasting deliverance, which is always the aim. You don't have to force a true manifestation, and a forced manifestation may not be a demonic manifestation at all.

It's okay to tell clients to breathe out if their chest feels tight. Breathing out is one way people expel demons. If you see the client shaking their hands, you might discern the demon came in through the sin of the hands. It's okay to tell the client to shake their hands free of the demons.

That said, don't coax a manifestation where there is not one. Don't push or require them to cough, for example, or burp. Be led by the Holy Spirit.

PROTOCOL 76
WHEN TO BIND MANIFESTATIONS

I f a person begins manifesting demons as the demon leaves, as long as it's not dangerous, we typically allow those manifestations. Here's why: Many times demons do cause some physical reaction when they come out. That may be the wringing of the hands, crying, coughing, vomiting, screaming, etc.

We're not trying to stop people from crying or coughing or vomiting. We want them to expel the demons. Jesus allowed a manifestation in Luke 4:3336:

"Now in the synagogue there was a man who had a spirit of an unclean demon. And he cried out with a loud voice, saying, 'Let us alone! What have we to do with You, Jesus of Nazareth? Did You come to destroy us? I know who You are— the Holy One of God!'

"But Jesus rebuked him, saying, 'Be quiet, and come out of him!' And when the demon had thrown him in their midst, it came out of him and did not hurt him. Then they were all amazed and spoke among themselves, saying, 'What a word this is! For with authority and power He commands the unclean spirits, and they come out.'"

Notice how Jesus forbade the demon to speak but did not stop the demon from throwing the man down. The demon, though, did come out without hurting the man.

That said, there are some manifestations you do want to bind, such as when the demonized client is engaging in any form of self-harm. You also always want to bind the mocking spirit. The mocking spirit may manifest as an evil smile, someone putting their fingers in their ears or mimicking you. You also want to bind, if it manifests, the slumbering spirit. Always bind spirits that get in the way of the client's freedom.

Moreover, you want to bind manifestations that could end up harming the deliverance ministers physically or drive fear, such as physical advances toward a minister, spitting, cussing, threats and the like. Just bind it up in Jesus name!

PROTOCOL 77
DEALING WITH DEMONIC TONGUES

How do you deal with demonic tongues? First, you have to discern them. Demonic tongues sound different than your gift of tongues you use to build yourself up in your most holy faith, according to Jude 20.
Demonic tongues have a different sound. They sound sinister and aggressive. They are often far more advanced than your tongues for edification, almost as if it's a demonic language. The Bible does speak of tongues of angels in 1 Corinthians 13:1. Considering demons are fallen angels, they speak in a perverted angelic tongue.

When you hear demonic tongues, you may get an eerie feeling, the hairs on the back of your neck may stand up, or you may get goosebumps or chills. Often, but not always, demonic tongues come along with some other manifestation in the context of deliverance, such as slumbering or aggressive behavior.

You deal with demonic tongues by binding them—forbidding them. You say, "I forbid you from speaking, in Jesus' name."

PROTOCOL 78
IF YOU HIT A WALL

If you hit a wall during the session, stop and pray. Don't keep trying to cast out a devil that's clearly not coming out. As mentioned earlier, you often can't deal with the strongman until you deal with the guards. The client will lose confidence in the process if you don't shift your strategy when you hit a wall.

Sometimes the spirit of counsel will come upon you, or you will receive a word of wisdom or a word of knowledge. Sometimes you'll know or feel something by the Spirit. But you have to stop long enough to sense His leadership. Jesus' disciples could not cast out the spirit from a boy.

Mark 9:17-18 reads, "Then one of the crowd answered and said, 'Teacher, I brought You my son, who has a mute spirit. And wherever it seizes him, it throws him down; he foams at the mouth, gnashes his teeth, and becomes rigid. So I spoke to Your disciples, that they should cast it out, but they could not.'"

You don't want people leaving your deliverance ministry telling others that you could not cast out the devil. Sometimes you have to regroup, pray and wait on the Lord for what to do next. The Holy Spirit will lead you and guide you into the truth that sets the captive free (see John 16:13).

Also, remember to rely on your team. You don't have to have all the prophetic insight and discernment. That's why you have a team. Ask the others if they are picking up on anything. If you bear witness to it, let them lead the charge in casting out the demon they discerned.

PROTOCOL 79

DON'T PLAY GUESSING GAMES OR MAKE ASSUMPTIONS

When you hit a wall, it can be tempting to assume and presume based on past experience instead of relying on the Holy Spirit. Don't do this. Deliverance is not rooted in deduction. It's not a guessing game. Effective deliverance ministry does not make assumptions or presumptions about a client.

Remember demons don't always play by the rule book and guessing can bring the client more harm than good. You can lose the confidence of the client, which hinders their faith to receive from you. Your team can lose confidence in you if it appears you are swinging randomly and missing. Even if the last 100 times you cast out fear and it went a certain way, don't assume different issues can't arise in the next session.

It's okay to acknowledge to the client that you've gone as far as you can go and that you and your team will go back into prayer and reschedule another session at a later time. Continuing to take shots in the dark is just stirring up the demonic realm for no reason.

It's also possible that the client is hiding something from you and you are not discerning it. If the client is hiding sin, you will hit a wall quickly or they may seem to get delivered but come back with the same issues a month later because they could not maintain their deliverance.

If they are hiding issues, they are not serious about getting delivered and you can't do anything about it. Even if you confront the client, they may not admit what they are hiding. It goes back to the client wanting to be free and cooperating with the process.

PROTOCOL 80
MAINTAIN PRIVACY IN
PUBLIC SETTINGS

Use privacy drapes when conducting deliverance in public, such as at a mass deliverance service, when someone manifests in a prayer line at the altar, or in other public settings in the church. By privacy drapes, I mean sheets of cloth that you use at the altar to cover people's bodies.

Have two or three people stand with curtains or a blanket if your client's body parts have been exposed. Preserve the dignity of the person by covering them. Deliverance is not a show. You may notice people will try to come around and watch. Don't let them.

PROTOCOL 81
FAN THE CLIENT

In extremely intense deliverance sessions in which the client has gone down to the ground, they may overheat. Have someone ready with a hand fan to fan the person who may be incapacitated during deliverance. You can even use a piece of paper. Anything that cools them down and lets them catch some air.

PROTOCOL 82
DON'T LET THE CLIENT LIE
ON THEIR FACE

In intense deliverance sessions where the client falls to the ground, don't let them lay flat on their face because they won't be able to breathe well. Remember they're not always cognizant during a deliverance ministry session. Sometimes, they are lying on their face because the demon doesn't want to look you in the eye. They want to hide their face.

The best position for someone who falls to the ground during deliverance is on their side. In this way, if they vomit they don't choke. If they go down, roll them over on their side and begin to fan them. And once they are aware and responsive, sit them up.

PROTOCOL 83
TELL THE CLIENT TO LEAVE
THEIR EYES OPEN

The enemy will often influence the client to close their eyes during the deliverance session. Sometimes that's because the enemy entered through the eyes and must come out through the eyes. Other times, it's a slumbering spirit trying to put the client to sleep. Still other times, the person is just uncomfortable. It's important that the client keep their eyes open unless they are incapacitated and are not in control.

PROTOCOL 84
DON'T MAKE DELIVERANCE
A COMPETITION

Don't compete with other deliverance ministers on the team. Follow the leader. Don't showboat. Competition breeds strife. If someone feels the need to show off in deliverance ministry, they are not ready to be on the team. They need to deal with some character issue or may themself need deliverance. Strife kills the anointing. The deliverance team must be in unity and working together.

Philippians 2:3-4 warns, "Let nothing be done through selfish ambition or conceit, but in lowliness of mind let each esteem others better than himself. Let each of you look out not only for his own interests, but also for the interests of others." Deliverance team members who cannot submit to the leader are out of order and can get in the way of the client's breakthrough.

PROTOCOL 85
YOU MAY NEED MORE
THAN ONE SESSION

You can't always cast out all the demons in one session. A person can only take so much. The Lord knows what the client can handle and how much deliverance they can successfully walk out. Even physically, the client can only take so much and the deliverance ministers can become exhausted as well. You need to discern when the Holy Spirit has gone as far as He is going to go and conclude the session.

PROTOCOL 86
CONSULT WITH EXPERTS IF NEEDED

Ethical deliverance ministers consult other experts when they hit a roadblock in releasing someone into freedom in Christ. Just like we know in part and prophesy in part, sometimes we don't see the whole demonic landscape in a client's case.

We may not have experience dealing with a certain issue or class of demons. In the medical world, surgeons have specialties and often confer with others in a different specialty in what's called a consult. It's the responsible thing to do. Nobody has all the answers.

PROTOCOL 87
REFER CLIENTS OUT IF NECESSARY

Ethical deliverance ministers refer clients to other deliverance specialists if they have exhausted their own ability to help them. There is no shame in that. Sometimes you are too close to a person or situation. Sometimes you don't have a high enough ranking or experience or revelation.

Sometimes you just can't get someone free, but you know someone who can. The right thing to do is admit when you don't have the skillset to walk someone through to freedom and recommend someone else, even if it's in another city, who can.

PROTOCOL 88
IMMEDIATE FOLLOW UP CARE

Immediately after a one-on-one deliverance session, we need to provide some follow up care and instructions. If it's been a long or aggressive session, the client is likely to be thirsty, hungry and worn out. Have tissues, water and even a protein bar on hand to take care of their physical body after this spiritual encounter. This is scriptural. Luke 8:49-55 reads:

"While He was still speaking, someone came from the ruler of the synagogue's house, saying to him, 'Your daughter is dead. Do not trouble the Teacher.'

"But when Jesus heard it, He answered him, saying, 'Do not be afraid; only believe, and she will be made well.' When He came into the house, He permitted no one to go in except Peter, James, and John, and the father and mother of the girl. Now all wept and mourned for her; but He said, 'Do not weep; she is not dead, but sleeping.' And they ridiculed Him, knowing that she was dead.

"But He put them all outside, took her by the hand and called, saying, 'Little girl, arise.' Then her spirit returned, and she arose immediately. And He commanded that she be given something to eat."

PROTOCOL 89
POST-DELIVERANCE QUESTIONS

Take the time after the deliverance session to answer any questions the client may have and counsel them on how to walk out their deliverance. Specifically ask them if they have questions. They may or may not, but it's important to give them the opportunity because they may not ask if you don't offer.

You may also feel compelled to discuss or explain what happened during the deliverance session. The goal is to help prevent enemy attacks on their mind about what took place. If they have questions, answer them because the devil will provide answers if you don't.

PROTOCOL 90
WARN ABOUT RETALIATION

It's critical that you warn the client what to expect with regard to retaliation. The enemy may tell them the deliverance was not successful. They may hear a voice that says, "You are not free" or something similar. Warn them how the enemy will try to come back in if they don't guard their minds. Jesus warned in Matthew 12:43-45:

"When an unclean spirit goes out of a man, it passes through dry places seeking rest, but finds none. Then it says, 'I will return to my house from which I came.' And when it comes, it finds it empty, swept, and put in order. Then it goes and brings with itself seven other spirits more evil than itself, and they enter and dwell there. And the last state of that man is worse than the first."

PROTOCOL 91
ENCOURAGE THE CLIENT
TO STAY PLUGGED IN TO CHURCH

The enemy loves to work in isolation. It's critical that the client stay connected to a local assembly and fellowship with believers. Hebrews 10:25 reads, "And let us not neglect our meeting together, as some people do, but encourage one another, especially now that the day of his return is drawing near." Post deliverance, clients need community.

PROTOCOL 92
GIVE THEM STEPS TO WALKING OUT THE DELIVERANCE

Beyond warning about retaliation, give the client steps to walking out their deliverance. We've created a brochure taking them through steps and suggestions, with Scriptures. You'll find this in the Appendix section.

PROTOCOL 93
IF NEEDED, SCHEDULE A FOLLOW UP

If you are aware more deliverance is required, schedule a follow-up session immediately after the current session, if possible. In this way, the client is more likely to continue on their journey to freedom. Try to schedule the next deliverance session a few weeks or a month later with the same team. If you need to add someone else to the team to deal with a specific issue, you will have time to plan that.

Don't let frustration, discouragement or disappointment hijack the client's journey to freedom. Remind them that deliverance often comes in layers and God knows how much they can walk out at any given time. Encourage them by letting them know they've made progress and leave them with a word of encouragement. Tell them what they can expect in the next session. Build up their faith for total freedom.

PROTOCOL 94
PRAY FOR CLIENT BEFORE ENDING

S ay a final prayer with the client before they leave to seal the deliverance and fill them with the Spirit. You never want to cast anything out without filling back up. Ask the Holy Spirit to seal the deliverance and fill them with the Spirit so that the empty places, now wiped clean, are filled up.

PROTOCOL 95
ESTABLISH A FOLLOW UP PROCESS

Just as oncologists have a follow-up process for cancer patients, deliverance ministries should have a follow up process for their clients.

You may need to call or email them in three days. You may tell them to call you if they start having any issues or questions. Stay committed to walking them through the deliverance after the session. Have a process in place, and this can look different depending on your ministry.

PROTOCOL 96
PRAY WITH YOUR TEAM AGAINST RETALIATION

When you cast out devils by the finger of God, then the Kingdom of God has come to you (Luke 11:20). But what comes next isn't always as much fun. There is often natural and spiritual retaliation for setting the captives free.

Although no weapon formed against a deliverance minister can prosper, the enemy nonetheless forms a weapon and takes his best shot. After all, when you cast out devils—when you set the captives free—you just did marked damage to the kingdom of darkness. Whether you are an experienced deliverance minister or just beginning to study the gospel art of casting out devils, entering the battle without expecting the backlash is not wise.

After Jesus cast the devil out of two demon-possessed men in the region of the Gadarenes, sending them into the swine, the entire town came out to meet Him. But instead of glorifying God as one might expect, they begged him to get out of town (see Matthew 8:22-33).

If that wasn't insulting enough, when Jesus cast a devil out of a blind and mute man, the Pharisees suggested He was using the power of Satan (see Matthew 12:24). And religious spirits were especially indignant that Jesus cast out a devil on the Sabbath day (see Luke 13:14).

Ultimately, one of the reasons the religious spirits wanted to kill Jesus was because he was setting people free from demonic oppression and, in doing so, threatening their dead religious rule.

Those who don't understand the spiritual dynamic of demonic oppression often criticize, mock or otherwise ridicule deliverance ministers. If you cast out devils, even some Christians may think you are a heretic or have a demon yourself. Such retaliation is from flesh and blood, but it is motivated by the whispers of the enemy who wants to persecute you sorely until you cast off your casting out ministry.

In his video teaching on Demonology & Deliverance, Lester Sumrall said he was greatly criticized for his teaching on casting out devils: "You've got to be able to accept that. If you are not able to accept that, the devil will defeat you quite easily. You've got to be willing to be mocked, to be laughed at, to be misunderstood in order to do what God wants you to do."

On the other side of the retaliation coin, deliverance ministers can expect retaliation through manifested spiritual warfare. I've cast devils out of people only to turn around and face a heavy dose of witchcraft or imaginations that tried to convince me the devil never left. I've had nightmares after exercising deliverance ministry. I've felt tired and sick. Thankfully, I understood that it was the enemy hitting back and took authority over the assignment in the name of Jesus.

When you set out to engage in deliverance ministry, don't go there without preparing your heart—and don't go there alone. Jesus sent the

72 disciples out two by two to cast out devils (see Matthew 10:8). And they understood their authority in the name of Jesus before they ventured into ministry. Deliverance ministry is not a game of patty cake.

To be sure, you can't just read *Pigs in the Parlor* and dub yourself a deliverance minister. If you don't truly understand your authority in Christ—if you don't have an intimate relationship with Him—the retaliation could be dramatic and painful. Remember the itinerant Jewish exorcists who took it upon themselves to call the name of the Lord Jesus over those who had evil spirits?

They said, "We exorcise you by the Jesus whom Paul preaches." The seven sons of Sceva joined into the deliverance party "And the evil spirit answered and said, 'Jesus I know, and Paul I know; but who are you?' Then the man in whom the evil spirit was leaped on them, overpowered them, and prevailed against them, so that they fled out of that house naked and wounded" (Acts 19:15-16).

Although you aren't likely to experience anything quite like what happened to the sons of Sceva, that doesn't mean you shouldn't prepare yourself for retaliation before you ever step foot into the deliverance session. Beyond fasting, seeking God for wisdom, and putting together a team of deliverance ministers, remember to bind up the retaliation and plead the blood of Jesus over yourself before and after the session. And everything you do, do it with faith in the name of Jesus. Amen.

Plead the blood of Jesus and pray for protection for the deliverance team after the session. Bind the retaliation. And wherever you are praying, cleanse the church after the deliverance session.

PROTOCOL 97
DEBRIEF WITH THE TEAM

Debriefing after a deliverance session is a must. It's a learning opportunity for the whole team. Everyone on the team has something to share, or perhaps questions to ask, or patterns to point out. You will want to let the trainee share what they wrote in their notes to see if they were discerning accurately. You want to discuss anything strange that may have happened and next steps if the person needs more deliverance.

PROTOCOL 98
DELIVERANCE MINISTER CHECKUPS

As deliverance ministers, you and your ministry team should maintain your own relationship with the Lord and your emotional health. You should walk in love but not fear as fear opens the door to the devil. You should have periodic spiritual checkups.

APPENDIX 1
DELIVERANCE INTAKE QUESTIONNAIRE

PERSONAL INFO
In this section, include spaces for the client's name, date, date of birth, phone number and email address, as well as gender, marital status and any other personal information you find useful.

SPIRITUAL BACKGROUND

Have you received deliverance for this issue in the past? If so, when, and with what ministry? Have you given your life to Christ? If yes, what was the approximate date? **Other questions:**

- Baptism of the Holy Spirit with evidence of speaking in tongues? If Yes, how often?
- How would you describe your current relationship with the Lord?
- Present and Past Church Affiliation:
- Please state the one current issue for which you would like to receive ministry. What is the most painful or difficult thing for you about this issue? What ways have you already tried to resolve this issue?
- How long has this impacted your life? List any similarities with painful situations in the more recent past.
- What does God say about this problem? Has it affected your relationship with God? If so, how?
- On a scale of 1-10 with 10 being excellent, rate your relationship with your Father?
- On a scale of 1-10 with 10 being excellent, rate your relationship with your Mother?
- The most important thing to me is...

- I worry about...
- I have sometimes felt guilty about..
- I have been criticized for...
- What makes me angry is...
- My biggest mistakes were...
- What makes me nervous is ...
- I often felt that mother...
- I often felt that father...
- God to me is...
- What hurts me most is...
- My biggest problem in life is...

OCCULT INVOLVEMENT

- Any PAST involvement? List things like astrology, astral projection, black magic, demon worship, divination, fortune telling, mediumship, mental telepathy, mind control, palm readings, pendulum readings, psychic readings, reincarnation, seances, sorcery, superstition, tarot cards, trance, white magic, witchcraft, voodoo, occult sex/ritual abuse, Buddhism, Christian Science, Eastern religions, Hinduism, Islam, Indian occult rituals, Jehovah's Witness, Mormonism, New Age, Satanic worship, spirit guides, scientology, shamanism, Shriners, Masons, spiritualism, Unitarian church, and Wicca

- Any CURRENT involvement? List the same as above
- Any GENERATIONAL (family) involvement? List the same as above
- What are the ethnic backgrounds of your ancestors? Were you adopted?
- Have you or your family ever been involved in a religion other than Christianity? If so, which one?

RELATIONAL QUESTIONS

- Have you or your family ever experienced any form of addiction, from drugs to alcohol to eating disorders? If so, please list them.
- Have you ever been depressed, anxious, suicidal or engaged in self-mutilating? If so, please explain. Have you ever experienced any sexual abuse, physical abuse or emotional abuse? If so, please explain? Have you ever experienced any form of trauma, such as accidents, or other live events that traumatized you? If so, please explain?
- Did you have a good relationship with your parents?
- Was your childhood happy?

- Have you, your spouse, parents or grandparents ever had serious medical issues? If so, please explain.
- Have you ever undergone psychological counseling?
- Do you suffer from nightmares or sleep disorders?
- Are you aware of any curse placed on your or your family?
- What are you afraid of?
- Have you ever been divorced or abandoned? If so, when?
- Do you have any unforgiveness or resentment toward anyone?
- What kinds of thoughts plague you?
- How would you describe your current relationship with your family?
- Are there other problems this questionnaire hasn't addressed? If so, please share.

PERSONAL HEALTH

Have you ever experienced any of the following? List things such as addictions of any kind, anxiety disorder, bipolar disorder, demonic dreams, disconnectedness, difficulties in relationships, eating disorders, major depression, hearing voices, mood swings, memory problems, sexual abuse, self-mutilation, severe headache, sleep disorders, out of body experience, obsessive compulsive disorder, sexual dysfunction (avoidance, addiction), unable to cope well with emotional stress.

- Any short-term or long-term illnesses in your body? If yes, list the illness and year of illness.
- Are you currently suffering from that illness?
- Please include any other information that is relevant to your current problem.

ADDITIONAL INFORMATION
Please include any other information that is relevant to your current problem.

APPENDIX 2
WAIVER OF CONFIDENTIALITY SAMPLE

I am aware that all statements that I should make to the Awakening House of Prayer are of confidential nature, including all written information, and that legally and ethically, these may not be disclosed without my written consent. However, I waive my right to "complete" confidentiality in the following situations:

1. I agree that my ministers may give a verbal or written summary report of the ministry to the Director of Deliverance Rooms and or their designated representatives concerning their ministry to me with the purpose of providing me with more effective ministry.

2. I accept and acknowledge that, Awakening House of Prayer, its leaders and deliverance ministers, or any other persons involved in working with adults and children in a helping setting, are either encouraged or required by law to disclose to the appropriate person, agency, or civil authority, any harm or potential harm that a person may attempt or desire to do to himself/herself or to others.

3. I accept and acknowledge that they are also required to report any reasonable suspicion of physical or sexual abuse that has been done, or that is being done to a minor child.

4. It is the policy of Awakening House of Prayer that any AHOP Member engaging in an ongoing sin that could represent a potential problem going forward, the Ministry Receiver

would waive confidentiality for this issue to be shared with the Church Leaders.

Signature _____

APPENDIX 3
WAIVER OF LIABILITY SAMPLE

I understand that I will be seeing Awakening House of Prayer Deliverance Ministers who will be able to listen, support, encourage, pray with, and minister to me to help me overcome problems and to grow in my Christian life.

I accept that they are not licensed counselors, that they minister by the Christian Bible, and that they may or may not be ordained and/or full time ministers.

I acknowledge that all ministry is under the direction and control of the Holy Spirit, and that no guarantees are made, nor can be made, by anyone or any organization that I will or will not receive any particular healing/ministry.

Thus I waive all rights to claim of liability. I accept that they may recommend further ministry for me by a pastor, counselor, home ministry group, support and/or other agencies where it could benefit me.

Signature _____

APPENDIX 4
AFTER CARE PROTOCOLS

Casting out devils. It's one of my favorite things to do because I love to see the Kingdom of God manifest. I love to see the power of God set the captives free. I love to see people loosed from oppression, depression, obsessions and all manner of sickness and disease. Jesus gave us authority to drive out demons (see Mark 3:15).

Just as surgeons give post-operative instructions, it's vital that we instruct people how to walk out or maintain their deliverance. Part of that process starts immediately after deliverance and part of it is up to the client to do the work to stay free.

Think about when you have surgery in the hospital. They put you in a recovery room before you go back to the hospital room. Even in outpatient surgery, they put you in a recovery room until you are stable enough to be transferred. The following is advice you can give to the client. You can print this out for your client with acknowledgement given to Awakening House of Prayer.

Practical Ways to Stay Free
If you were delivered from a spirit of fear, for example, meditate on Scriptures about how God has not given you a spirit of fear and Scriptures about the peace of God. If you were delivered from rejection, meditate on the love and acceptance of God. If you were delivered from lust, meditate on the holiness and purity and beauty of God. If you meditate on the Word day and night and carefully do what it says, you will find good success (see Josh. 1:8).

Be quick to cast down imaginations and voices that speak contrary to the Word of God (see 2 Corinthians 10:5). If you were delivered from a spirit of anger, be quick to recognize and resist voices and urges toward anger. If you were delivered from a spirit of infirmity, rebuke the symptoms—the Bible calls them lying vanities (see Jonah 2:8)—instead of accepting them. Ultimately, the key to lasting victory is to submit yourself to God and resist the devil and he will flee (see James 4:7).

Finally, keep worship music on in your home or your car. Listen to solid teaching CDs or MP3s that reinforce the freedom you are walking in. Develop a more intimate relationship with God. Fellowship with the Holy Spirit. Pray without ceasing. When you do these things, you'll walk in the reality that who the Son sets free is free indeed!

After your deliverance rooms session, you will walk away with a new measure of freedom. We are celebrating your freedom with you! It is our honor and passion to help you walk in the prophetic life of victory Jesus died and rose again to give you. Now, you have to walk out your deliverance. The days and week after your deliverance, you are vulnerable to demonic attacks.

Jesus said, "When an unclean spirit goes out of a man, it passes through dry places seeking rest, but finds none. Then it says, 'I will return to my house from which I came.' And when it comes, it finds it empty, swept, and put in order. Then it goes and brings with itself seven other spirits more evil than itself, and they enter and dwell there. And the last state of that man is worse than the first" (Matthew 12:43-45).

When you get delivered from a demon, that spirit will find a way to try to regain access to your life. Demons need a body through which to operate—and they're glad to take up residence in your vessel if you'll allow it. Don't allow it! You have to set your heart and mind against the enemy's moves to re-enter your life—and bring seven other spirits that are even more evil. How do you do this?

Peter strictly warned us, "Be well balanced (temperate, sober of mind), be vigilant and cautious at all times; for that enemy of yours, the devil, roams around like a lion roaring [in fierce hunger], seeking someone to seize upon and devour" (1 Peter 5:8, AMPC).

1. When you go home, do not engage in any entertainment or idle talk. Spend time with the Lord debriefing on what He showed you during your deliverance session. If you are too tired to do that, get something to eat and go to sleep. When you wake up in the morning, thank the Lord for the deliverance and study Scriptures that combat the lies the enemy oppressed you with. For example, if you were delivered from rejection or fear, study the love of God. Study the truth that combats the lies the enemy wrapped you up in.

2. Guard your mind. Watch your thoughts. The enemy will usually attempt to tell you the same lies again and again during the first week or two or even three after your deliverance. This is why it's so important to renew your mind with the Word of God. The truth encounter with the Holy Spirit set you free, but it's walking in that truth that will keep you free.

Test the voices (spirits) that you hear to see if they are from God (see 1 John 4:1). The voice of God is full of wisdom, peace, love and truth. Paul said, "whatever things are true, whatever things are noble, whatever things are just, whatever things are pure, whatever things are lovely, whatever things are of good report, if there is any virtue and if there is anything praiseworthy—meditate on these things" (Philippians 4:8).

3. Continue to plead the blood daily over your mind, will and emotions, as well as your physical body. You were redeemed and set free because of the shed blood of Jesus. Demons hate the blood and any talk of the blood.

4. Cultivate a habit of leaving worship music playing in your house or car, or a recording of the Bible.

5. At some point, the enemy may try to convince you that you were not delivered. Remember, your behavior may not completely change after you are set free because you still have to renew your mind and change your habits. A habit is different than a demon. When the enemy tells you that you aren't free, begin thanking the Lord for your freedom. Work with the Holy Spirit to create new habits.

6. Watch your words. The enemy will try to get you to confess that you are not delivered. The enemy will try to get you to curse yourself rather than bless yourself. Don't gossip, slander, or accuse others. Ask the Holy Spirit to help you tame your tongue (see James 3:8).

7. Pray for a hedge of protection around your house, your workplace, your church or wherever you go. Praying Psalm 91 is a good way to pray a hedge of protection.

8. Cleanse your home of any objects that could attract demon powers. Look through boxes and in closets to see if you have any objects depicting snakes, owls, turtles, or anything of the occult or witchcraft—even children's toys and movies.

9. Throw away any jewelry that may be attracting demon powers. That includes amulets, Catholic symbols, occult charms, etc.

10. Practice quick forgiveness, so you give no place to the devil (see Ephesians 4:27).

11. Ask the Lord to break deception off your mind.

12. Ask the Lord to fill you with His Spirit again every day (see Ephesians 5:8)

13. Yield to the Holy Spirit in every area of their life.

14. Dress in the armor of God every day.

15. Stay away from bad alignments.

16. Put Jesus at the center of your life (see John 12:31-32).

17. Wear the garment of praise (see Isaiah 61:3).

18. Pray in tongues as much as possible.

APPENDIX 4
ADDITIONAL RESOURCES

SCHOOL OF DELIVERANCE
You can find the School of Deliverance at www.schoolofthespirit.tv

SCHOOL OF SPIRITUAL WARFARE
You can find the School of Spiritual Warfare and other spiritual warfare courses at *www.schoolofthespirit.tv*

DEMONS & DEMONOLOGY
You can find the Demons & Demonology course at *www.schoolofthespirit.tv*

SELF-DELIVERANCE AUDIOS
You can find a list of self-deliverance audios to refer clients to for additional support at *youtube.com/jenniferleclaireministries*

NOTES

NOTES

ABOUT THE AUTHOR

JENNIFER LECLAIRE is an internationally recognized author, apostolic-prophetic voice to her generation, and conference speaker. She carries a reforming voice that inspires and challenges believers to pursue intimacy with God, cultivate their spiritual gifts and walk in the fullness of what God has called them to do. Jennifer is contending for awakening in the nations through intercession and spiritual warfare, strong apostolic preaching and practical prophetic teaching that equips the saints for the work of the ministry.

Jennifer is senior leader of Awakening House of Prayer in Fort Lauderdale, FL, founder of the Ignite Network and founder of the Awakening Prayer Hubs prayer movement.

Jennifer formerly served as the first-ever editor of *Charisma* magazine. Her work also appeared in a Charisma House book entitled *Understanding the Five-Fold Ministry* which offers a biblical study to uncover the true purpose for the fivefold ministry and *The Spiritual Warfare Bible*, which is designed to help you use the Bible to access the power of the Holy Spirit against demonic strongholds and activity. Some of Jennifer's work is also archived in the Flower Pentecostal Heritage Museum.

Jennifer is a prolific author who has written over 50 books, including. Some of her materials have been translated into Spanish and Korean.

Beyond her frequent appearances on the Elijah List, Jennifer writes one of *Charisma*'s most popular prophetic columns, *The Plumb Line*, and frequently contributes to *Charisma*'s Prophetic Insight newsletter. Her media ministry includes her website; 500,000 followers on Facebook, Twitter and YouTube. Jennifer has been interviewed on numerous media outlets including USA Today, BBC, CBN, The Alan Colmes Show, Bill Martinez Live, Babbie's House, Atlanta Live and Sid Roth's *It's Supernatural*, as well as serving as an analyst for Rolling Thunder Productions on a *Duck Dynasty* special presentation.

Jennifer also sits on the media advisory board of the *Hispanic Israel Leadership Coalition*.

OTHER BOOKS BY
JENNIFER LECLAIRE

Angels on Assignment Again

Decoding Your Dreams

Decoding the Mysteries of Heaven's War Room

The Prophet's Devotional

Decrees that Make the Devil Flee

Tongues of Fire

The Making of a Watchman

Cleansing Your Home from Evil

The Seer Dimensions

Seer Activations

Power Seers

Your Prayer Secret

Walking in Your Prophetic Destiny

Victory Decrees (devotional)

The Spiritual Warrior's Guide to Defeating Water Spirits

Releasing the Angels of Abundant Harvest

The Heart of the Prophetic

A Prophet's Heart

The Making of a Prophet

The Spiritual Warrior's Guide to Defeating Jezebel

Did the Spirit of God Say That?

Satan's Deadly Trio

Jezebel's Puppets

The Spiritual Warfare Battle Plan

Waging Prophetic Warfare

Dream Wild!

Faith Magnified

Fervent Faith

Breakthrough!

Mornings With the Holy Spirit

Evenings With the Holy Spirit

Revival Hubs Rising

The Next Great Move of God

Developing Faith for the Working of Miracles

You can download Jennifer's mobile apps by searching for "Jennifer LeClaire" in your app store and find Jennifer's podcasts on iTunes.

I BELIEVE IN PROPHETIC MINISTRY with every fiber of my being, but we all know the prophetic movement has seen its successes and failures. With an end times army of prophets and prophetic people rising up according to Joel 2:28 and Acts 2:17-20, it's more important than ever that we equip the saints for the work of prophetic ministry. Enter Ignite.

Ignite is a prophetic network birthed out of an encounter with the Lord that set a fire in my hearts to raise up a generation of prophets and prophetic people who flow accurately, operate in integrity, and pursue God passionately. I am laboring to cultivate a family of apostolic and prophetic voices and companies of prophets in the nations who can edify, comfort and exhort each other as we contend for pure fire in the next great move of God. My vision for Ignite covers the spiritual, educational, relational and accountability needs of five-fold ministers and intercessory prayer leaders.

You can learn more at *www.ignitenow.org*.

AWAKENING PRAYER HUBS PRAYER MOVEMENT

THE AWAKENING PRAYER HUBS mission in any city is to draw a diverse group of intercessors who have one thing in common: to contend for the Lord's will in its city, state and nation.

The vision of Awakening Prayer Hubs prayer spokes is to unite intercessors in cities across the nations of the earth to cooperate with the Spirit of God to see the second half of 2 Chronicles 7:14 come to pass: "If My people, who are called by My name, will humble themselves and pray, and seek My face and turn from their wicked ways, then I will hear from heaven, and will forgive their sin and will heal their land."

For many years, intercessors have been repenting, praying, and seeking God for strategies. Awakening Prayer Hubs intercessors will press into see the land healed, souls saved, churches established, ministries launched, and other Spirit-driven initiatives. Blaze intercessors will help undergird other ministries in their city, partnering with them in prayer where intercession may be lacking. Although *Awakening Prayer Hubs* are not being planted to birth churches, it is possible that

churches could spring up from these intercessory prayer cells if the Lord wills.
You can find out more about this prayer movement at *www.awakeningprayerhubs.com.*

You can also join the Awakening House Church Movement at:

http://www.awakeninghouse.com

Or plant a house of prayer via Awakening House of Prayer at:

http://www.awakeninghouseofprayer.com/startahouseofprayer